Cambridge Elements

Elements in Race, Ethnicity, and Politics
edited by
Megan Ming Francis
University of Washington

AF588173

WHICH LIVES MATTER?

Factors Shaping Public Attention to and Protest of Officer-Involved Killings

Traci Burch
Northwestern University and the American Bar Foundation

CAMBRIDGE
UNIVERSITY PRESS

Shaftesbury Road, Cambridge CB2 8EA, United Kingdom

One Liberty Plaza, 20th Floor, New York, NY 10006, USA

477 Williamstown Road, Port Melbourne, VIC 3207, Australia

314–321, 3rd Floor, Plot 3, Splendor Forum, Jasola District Centre, New Delhi – 110025, India

103 Penang Road, #05–06/07, Visioncrest Commercial, Singapore 238467

Cambridge University Press is part of Cambridge University Press & Assessment, a department of the University of Cambridge.

We share the University's mission to contribute to society through the pursuit of education, learning and research at the highest international levels of excellence.

www.cambridge.org
Information on this title: www.cambridge.org/9781009454377

DOI: 10.1017/9781108982870

© Traci Burch 2023

This publication is in copyright. Subject to statutory exception and to the provisions of relevant collective licensing agreements, no reproduction of any part may take place without the written permission of Cambridge University Press & Assessment.

First published 2023

A catalogue record for this publication is available from the British Library

ISBN 978-1-009-45437-7 Hardback
ISBN 978-1-108-98729-5 Paperback
ISSN 2633-0423 (online)
ISSN 2633-0415 (print)

Additional resources for this publication at www.cambridge.org/burch.

Cambridge University Press & Assessment has no responsibility for the persistence or accuracy of URLs for external or third-party internet websites referred to in this publication and does not guarantee that any content on such websites is, or will remain, accurate or appropriate.

Which Lives Matter?

Factors Shaping Public Attention to and Protest of Officer-Involved Killings

Elements in Race, Ethnicity, and Politics

DOI: 10.1017/9781108982870
First published online: September 2023

Traci Burch
Northwestern University and the American Bar Foundation

Author for correspondence: Traci Burch, t-burch@northwestern.edu

Abstract: This Element explores the factors that lead the public to pay attention to and mobilize in support of victims of officer-involved killings. The author argues that race is the most important factor shaping both attention and mobilization. Black victims are statistically significantly more likely to trend on Google and get protested than victims of other races. Deaths of low threat Black victims are more likely to affect political interest, voter turnout, and protest rates, and only among young Black observers. This Element attributes this pattern to the fact that mobilization around officer-involved killings is responding to anti-Black discrimination, rather than general sentiments about police violence. It also finds that the local density of social justice organizations increases political mobilization.

Keywords: political behavior, protest, social movements, policing, voter turnout

© Traci Burch 2023

ISBNs: 9781009454377 (HB), 9781108987295 (PB), 9781108982870 (OC)
ISSNs: 2633-0423 (online), 2633-0415 (print)

Contents

> My brother Matthew Tucker didn't get a video. He didn't get a hashtag. He didn't get human dignity from the police. And he didn't get to see his 19th birthday.
>
> Michael Shawn Tucker, in *The Washington Post* (Tucker 2020)

1 Introduction

On May 25, 2020, four Minneapolis police officers arrested George Floyd based on allegations that he tried to pass a counterfeit twenty-dollar bill, which turned out to be real (Hill et al. 2020). Officer Derek Chauvin was videotaped kneeling on Mr. Floyd's neck for over eight minutes during the arrest (Hill et al. 2020). Mr. Floyd died. All four officers were charged in his death, and Mr. Chauvin was convicted of murder for his actions. Mr. Floyd's killing was not the first incident in recent history in which an unarmed person was killed by police in the Minneapolis area: Philando Castile was killed by the St. Anthony, Minnesota police department in 2016, and a Minneapolis police officer also killed Justine Damond in 2017 (Forliti 2019).

As a result of Mr. Floyd's death, public outrage over police violence boiled over into the streets at a record pace. The protests were large and sustained. The Armed Conflict Location and Event Data Project (ACLED) examined 7,750 demonstrations that took place between Floyd's death on May 25 and August 22, 2020 (ACLED 2020). They found that demonstrations against police brutality took place in 2,400 places (ACLED 2020). Almost all of these demonstrations, 93 percent, were peaceful, which the ACLED defines as having no reports of property damage or violence (ACLED 2020). Surveys estimate between fifteen and twenty-six million people attended at least one of these protests even in the midst of a deadly pandemic (Buchanan, Bui, and Patel 2020). This figure represents up to 10 percent of American adults (Buchanan, Bui, and Patel 2020).

Not every victim,[1] however, of officer-involved killings attracts the attention and outrage that George Floyd did. Many deaths go unnoticed, and unprotested, by the public. Breonna Taylor, a young woman killed by Louisville police as she slept in her bed because of a no-knock warrant that police mistakenly served at her home, failed to garner either local or national attention until George Floyd died several months after she did (Conn 2020). As one protester of Taylor's death admitted, "'Honestly, . . . I didn't even know about her until I came out here to protest. . . . But at first, . . . I was out here protesting for George'" (Conn 2020). Similarly, as his brother notes in the opening quote, Matthew Tucker was killed by police in 2016 but his death was protested only after activists rediscovered his case in the wake of George Floyd's death four years later (Tucker 2020).

[1] Throughout this Element, the term "victim" is used to refer to people killed in officer-involved incidents. This convention follows medical and epidemiological conventions that refer to victims of particular causes of death without regard to notions of desert or culpability.

Countless other victims remain invisible to the public (Massie 2016; Ryan 2016), generating neither viral attention nor public backlash.

Still other deaths at the hands of police officers go viral immediately, yet fail to spark a public mobilization even close to the outpouring that occurred after the death of George Floyd. Even when the victim is Black, Threadcraft writes, "it has become clear that all black bodies do not produce equal amounts of community outrage" (Threadcraft 2017: 557). For instance, the death of Ma'Khia Bryant, a sixteen-year-old who was shot by Columbus, Ohio police in the spring of 2021, was widely discussed in the news and on social media. However, "some of the same people who called for justice in [George] Floyd's case" were not doing so for Bryant, largely because she was armed and fighting another woman when she was killed (Cineas 2021).

Based on the years of public agitation surrounding officer-involved killings, the public clearly pays attention to and protests these incidents in many circumstances. But then, the question becomes, why do some cases motivate and mobilize the public and not others? Despite the fact that officer-involved killings have sparked such an important social movement, very little work attempts to explain the circumstances that lead the public to pay attention to particular victims, or to protest some deaths, and not others.

This Element explores the factors that lead the public to pay attention to and mobilize in response to particular officer-involved deaths. It relies on data on officer-involved killings from FatalEncounters.org, combined with an original collection of additional variables about each of the victims of officer-involved killings that took place in 2016. I also explore the political behavior of survey respondents who live in close proximity to officer-involved killings. These data allow for the examination of attention and mobilization from the perspective of victims as well as from that of observers.

I find that attention and mobilization are driven by different processes. For Black people, I theorize that the pattern of attention to and mobilization against officer-involved killings should be understood not as a movement against generalized state violence, or even as a movement protesting violence against Black people, but as a backlash against a larger system of anti-Black discrimination. Unlike other racial groups,[2] Black people are overrepresented among victims of officer-involved killings, and their deaths, particularly those

[2] African American men and women face the highest lifetime risk of death at the hands of an officer (Edwards, Esposito, and Lee 2019), and according to the data I analyze here, only African Americans and Native Americans are overrepresented among victims of officer-involved killings relative to their share of the adult population. However, there are only twenty-nine Native Americans and twenty-five Asians in the data.

which cannot be explained by legally relevant factors such as threatening behavior by the victim, are more likely to generate public attention and mobilization among Black people than deaths of people of other races. Officer-involved killings, then, are most likely to provoke mobilization when they are constructed as motivated by anti-Black bias. By this logic, killings of Black people that are not clearly motivated by racial animus, and killings of non-Black victims in general, should not mobilize a public backlash. By extension, killings of Black people should be more likely to mobilize groups who, because of proximity or threat, are more concerned about anti-Black discrimination.

The data support this theory: race is the primary factor that explains mobilization around officer-involved killings. Race also is a significant predictor of public attention to officer-involved killings. As shown by my analysis of victims of officer-involved killings in this Element, Black victims statistically are significantly most likely to receive public attention and visibility (which I define as trending on Google) and to get protested. Moreover, my analyses of people living in close proximity to officer-involved killings shows that only deaths of Black victims affect political interest, voter turnout, and protest, and they do so only among young Black observers. At both the victim and observer levels, only deaths of Black victims who were not posing a threat to bystanders or officers were mobilizing, suggesting that the lack of a legally relevant explanation for police violence matters to people who are considering mobilizing. However, the threat level of the decedent is not related to the level of public attention their death receives.

I find that other factors also affect public attention and protest. Incident characteristics matter: people are statistically significantly more likely to pay attention to and protest when police kill people with guns and when a recording is available, and less likely to protest when victims die in car accidents (but car accidents are not statistically significant predictors of trending). Victim characteristics also matter: older people are statistically significantly less likely to trend on Google and to have their deaths protested when they are killed by police, while women statistically are significantly more likely to trend on Google (but not to get protested). Native American victims also are more likely to have their deaths protested; however, these numbers may be unreliable because the number of victims is very small. Finally, the presence of social justice organizations in the community statistically significantly increases the likelihood that a victim's death will generate both public attention and protest. I argue that the effect of social justice organizations operates through their important role in publicizing, framing, and organizing the response to incidents.

1.1 Theory and Plan of the Element

The 2020 protests of George Floyd's death were unprecedented in their size, scope, and duration (Buchanan, Bui, and Patel 2020), but they were not unusual. Instances of police violence have triggered periodic uprisings across the country for decades, especially when victims were unarmed and Black. The 1991 beating of Rodney King by four police officers spurred the subsequent 1992 riots that rocked Los Angeles when all four officers were acquitted of the charges they faced. Other instances of police violence against Abner Louima and Amadou Diallo spurred protests as well. However, it was the 2014 shooting of unarmed Black teenager Michael Brown by police officer Darren Wilson that brought police violence to the forefront of national consciousness and placed it at the center of a sustained, mass movement (Cobb 2016). Additional incidents, such as the police shootings of Laquan McDonald (October 2014), Tamir Rice (November 2014), Walter Scott (April 2015), Alton Sterling (July 2016), Philando Castile (July 2016), Keith Scott (September 2016), and Stephon Clark (2018) and the deaths in police custody of Eric Garner (July 2014), Freddie Gray (April 2015), and Sandra Bland (July 2015) further enhanced attention to police violence even before George Floyd was killed.

Scholarly evidence suggests that police violence leads to mobilization. The most famous document to link problem policing to the mobilization of Black protest in particular is perhaps the 1968 Kerner Report. More recent evidence supports the notion that aggressive policing practices, such as stop, question, and frisk or the use of lethal force, can mobilize the public. Williamson, Trump, and Einstein find that Black Lives Matter protests are more likely to occur in cities where police have previously shot Black people (Williamson, Trump, and Einstein 2018). Laniyonu finds that New York City areas that were more exposed to stop, question, and frisk voted at higher rates in both general and municipal elections and were more likely to support candidates who were opposed to the practice (Laniyonu 2019). Walker (2014) and Owens and Walker (2018) find that contact with the criminal justice system increases participation in nonvoting political activities as well (Owens and Walker 2018; Walker 2014).

However, even with the expectation that police violence can lead to protest and other forms of political participation, the literature does not explain when and under what circumstances such mobilization might occur. There are many people killed in officer-involved incidents who "didn't get a hashtag," media attention, or a protest (Tucker 2020). The existing literature on social movements can be useful for understanding when and why people turn to political action to achieve their goals.

Political opportunity or political process models focus on the political context, not just the resources and attitudes of aggrieved individuals, to explain mobilization (Meyer 2004). Political activity is costly, and the barriers to collective action can be difficult to overcome. However, mobilization does occur, and broadly speaking, political opportunity models focus on three factors to explain why: the development of a grievance, the organizational capacity and resources of aggrieved groups, and the structure of political opportunities available to the group (Meyer 2004). Political opportunity models are particularly useful for understanding the dynamics that affect social movements; however, they have some shortcomings. In particular, such models are not very good at predicting or explaining when mobilization might occur, or even change over time in the level of engagement and mobilization. Typically, changes such as escalation or disruption are explained in light of changes to the openness of the political system, or the availability of resources. The first factor, grievances, is less central to the understanding of how movements unfold over time.

However, in Section 2, I focus on the first component of political opportunity models, grievances, as the most important for understanding mobilization in response to officer-involved killings. Two critical factors influence the likelihood that an officer-involved death will develop into a grievance sufficient to mobilize public backlash: the visibility and traceability of the incident (Pierson 1993). These factors are vitally important, and without them, punishing government actors for an outcome "becomes virtually impossible" (Arnold 1990: 48). In Section 2, I argue that officer-involved killings are particularly visible to young Black people because of their proximity to such incidents; they are more likely to know about them because of their networks as well as because of increased surveillance. I also discuss the traceability of officer-involved killings to government fault; specifically, whether such killings can be attributed to legally relevant factors such as victim behavior rather than accidents, mistakes, or even racial bias. I argue that traceability to racial bias determines whether a killing will generate attention and mobilization.

Section 3 presents the data and discusses several data analyses. First, I provide a broad overview of the victims of officer-involved killings for one year, 2016. I relate victim and incident characteristics such as race, gender, and manner of death to the likelihood of public attention and protest. I show that race affects both public attention and protest; Black victims are more likely to receive public attention and protest. However, I also show the importance of grievance: low-threat victims are most likely to be protested. Finally, I confirm these victim-level findings at the observer level: low-threat Black victims are more likely to mobilize political interest and voter turnout than other groups, and only among young Black victims. Finally, I finish with a discussion of protest at the observer level.

Section 4 discusses an additional factor in the political process model: the role of organizations. In this section, I theorize about the importance of organizational capacity and social networks for mobilization against officer-involved killings, highlighting the importance of activists and social justice organizations. Social justice activists and organizations are particularly important for tying these deaths to a larger social movement for Black liberation, and their activities shape public attention and protest by publicizing Black victims of officer-involved killings and mobilizing the public. In line with this argument, I find that community resources, especially organizational capacity, are associated with both public attention and protest. The density of social justice organizations in a city, or of social justice organizations per capita, is positively associated with whether a victim trends on Google and gets protested. At most levels of social justice organizational density, this effect is modest; however, attention and protest in cities with very high densities of social justice organization were almost certain for some victims. Other measures of resources, such as local poverty, do not have a statistically significant association with protest, but do dampen the likelihood that a victim will trend on Google.

In Section 5, I conclude with a further discussion of the implications of this Element. I focus not only on the implications for political actors such as police departments and activists, but also on the implications for future research on the mobilizing effects of officer-involved killings. For government actors, I argue that the politics of officer-involved killings I have highlighted here create incentives to actively obfuscate the use of force by police and construct victims of officer-involved killings as dangerous. For activists, I focus on the obstacles to building a larger, cross-racial movement against racial discrimination *and* police violence. And for researchers, I discuss the importance of accounting for race, threat, and other factors when analyzing the effects of officer-involved killings on politics.

1.2 Contributions

One of the most important contributions of this Element is to collect empirical evidence to answer the questions of "mobilization *for whom*?" and "mobilization *by whom*?" with respect to the mass mobilization against officer-involved killings. Understanding the factors that shape responses to particular victims is critical for evaluating the public's likelihood of holding government officials, particularly mayors, prosecutors, and police chiefs, responsible for problems in their police departments. As this Element will demonstrate, most people who are killed in officer-involved incidents will not receive public attention or a protest. Most of their families will not receive settlements and many of the officers involved will not suffer long-term damage to their careers as a result of the incident (Lalwani 2020; Ray 2020; Stinson, Liederbach, and Brewer Jr. 2016). The inequality in who gets public attention and protest should matter if one thinks that attention and mobilization can lead to civil or criminal court resolutions or other forms of accountability in particular cases.

Understanding how crucial the development of grievances is for mobilization against officer-involved killings clarifies the importance of government transparency to accountability. Police and government actors sometimes attempt to reduce transparency surrounding the details of officer-involved killings, and, as this Element shows, those actions matter. As a clear example of this point, many political observers accuse Chicago mayor Rahm Emanuel of covering up the 2014 Laquan McDonald killing by Chicago police for political gain, out of fear that the public backlash and protest that took place in similar incidents in other cities would cost him reelection if it happened in Chicago (Harcourt 2015). The brother of Matthew Tucker also argues that his family was threatened with lawsuits for talking publicly about his brother's death (Tucker 2020). By showing the importance of visibility to mobilization, the role of government actions to obscure these incidents from the public becomes important to explaining why public backlash took months, or years, to develop in these cases.

I also show that officer-involved killings have important effects for democracy. Officer-involved killings increase political interest and mobilize young Black people to protest and vote in the face of police actions that they construct as unjust. Black youth electoral participation has been increasing in recent elections (Rogowski and Cohen 2015); this Element offers heightened attention to police violence as an additional mechanism driving political participation for a new generation of Black youth.

This Element highlights the importance of activists and social justice organizations for accountability as well. As I will discuss, such organizations publicize incidents and produce counternarratives of victims of officer-involved killings. They also help solve collective action and other problems of organizing. Section 4 demonstrates the importance of this finding at the micro level; communities without this infrastructure are less likely to respond to officer-involved killings.

Finally, this Element contributes to the study of social movements by highlighting the explanatory power of grievances, at least with respect to the Movement for Black Lives. The theory presented here combines insights of the Kerner Commission with those of contemporary social movement scholars. I argue that grievances change over time, at least in terms of salience and meaning. I discuss this claim in more detail in the next section.

2 Grievances and Mobilization against Officer-Involved Killings

Grievances play an important role in mobilizing political action. According to Felstiner, Abel, and Sarat (1980), a grievance occurs when a "perceived injurious experience" is attributed "to the fault of another individual or social entity" (Felstiner, Abel, and Sarat 1980: 635). McAdam also argues that "cognitive liberation" is a precursor to social movements and occurs when "a significant segment of the aggrieved population" views "their situations as unjust and subject to change through group action" (McAdam 1982: 51). Inherent in these definitions are two critical factors: an injury must be visible or perceived as such and some entity must be assigned responsibility for perpetrating it (Pierson 1993).

In this section, I explore the concept of grievances, arguing that these two characteristics of grievances, which Paul Pierson labels visibility and traceability, are the most important factors for understanding who and when officer-involved killings will mobilize (Pierson 1993). I argue that officer-involved killings are more likely to mobilize the public when they are visible. Moreover, killings are more likely to mobilize when they are perceived as an injury or threat, which occurs when they are traceable to government wrongdoing.

As I will argue, the type of wrongdoing that is mobilizing political action in response to officer-involved killings is not a generalized concern about police violence, but instead a concern about anti-Black discrimination. I argue that mobilizations against officer-involved killings are defensive mobilizations in response to racial threat. For this reason, the race of observers and the race and behavior of victims should be important to the visibility and traceability of a given incident. I rely on Soss and Schram's notion of proximity (Soss and Schram 2007) to show that officer-involved killings should be particularly visible to young Black people: they are more likely to be killed by police and they are more likely to know about incidents because of their networks as well as because of increased surveillance. I also discuss the traceability of officer-involved killings to government fault; in particular, whether such killings can be attributed to legally relevant factors such as victim behavior rather than accidents, mistakes, or racial bias. I argue that traceability to racial bias may activate anger among many observers, but is most likely to activate a sense of threat, which can be mobilizing, among young Black observers. This insight, that anger over anti-Black discrimination shapes mobilization and attention to officer-involved killings, sets up the expectation that only certain killings, those that can be attributed to anti-Black racism, will generate a public response.

2.1 Officer-Involved Killings, the Racialization of Grievance, and Mobilization

Dating back to the 1968 Kerner Report, policing often has been called out as a "perceived injurious experience," or grievance, that can mobilize Black political engagement. Public opinion research consistently has found that police-related grievances, or the extent to which the public views police and police actions as a problem, vary by race even today. Grievances against police and the criminal justice system more broadly are held more commonly by Black Americans than any other group. For instance, racial gaps exist in beliefs about police use of force: 42 percent of White respondents believe that their local police do an "excellent" or "good" job of using the right amount of force, but only 29 percent of Latino and 11 percent of Black respondents feel that way (Pew Research Center 2020). Two-thirds of White people think that their local police do an "excellent" or "good" job of protecting people from crime, compared with 50 percent of Latino and 28 percent of Black people (Pew Research Center 2020).

Perceptions of anti-Black discrimination by the criminal justice system generally, and by police in particular, also vary by race. Countless studies have shown that Black Americans perceive the criminal justice system in general and police specifically as unfair and racially discriminatory, while other groups, especially White Americans, are less likely to perceive bias (Bobo and Johnson 2004; Hurwitz and Peffley 2001, 2005; Johnson 2008; Johnson and Kuhns 2009; Peffley and Hurwitz 2010; Peffley and Jon 2002). Forty-two percent of White respondents also think that their local police do an "excellent" or "good" job of treating racial and ethnic groups equally, compared with only 26 percent of Latino and 9 percent of Black respondents (Pew Research Center 2020). Gallup argues that the racial gap in confidence in police between Black and White respondents is the largest found for any of the sixteen institutions they included in their survey (Jones 2020).

Research has shown that these perceptions stem from racial differences in negative experiences with police such as aggression and poor service. Scholars argue that "violations of one racial group by the other" such as rape, murder, assault, and police brutality (Lieberson and Silverman 1965), and police brutality specifically (Bergesen 1982), are responsible for the urban unrest of the 1960s and 1970s. Today, Black people are more likely to be stopped and searched by police and to report negative encounters with them (Epp, Maynard-Moody, and Haider-Markel 2014; Gelman, Fagan, and Kiss 2007; Lundman and Kaufman 2003; Pierson et al. 2020). In addition to violence and harassment, inadequate service also plays a role in dissatisfaction with police and with urban unrest. The Kerner Report even notes that responses to demands for better service in Black communities are met with more aggressive policing, which makes the problem worse (Kerner and Lindsay 1968). Skogan also finds that Black Chicago residents persistently voice concerns about inadequate service as well (Skogan 2006).

Over time, such experiences can lead to McAdam's "cognitive liberation." However, the process through which problems become perceived as injustice that is remediable through by action is not triggered immediately in response to any isolated incident. Rather, the perception develops over the long term. Explaining urban unrest in the 1960s, the Kerner Report notes, "Disorder did not erupt as a result of a single 'triggering' or 'precipitating' incident. Instead, it was generated out of an increasingly disturbed social atmosphere, in which typically a series of tension-heightening incidents over a period of weeks or months became linked in the minds of many in the Negro community with a reservoir of underlying grievances" (Kerner and Lindsay 1968). The Kerner Report notes that prior incidents with police "increased tensions and ultimately led to violence" and in half of events also "became the breaking point" that led to violence (Kerner and Lindsay 1968). In the contemporary period, activists acknowledge that "protests in Milwaukee, Baltimore, and Ferguson stemmed not just from a police killing, but also from decades of neglecting entire communities" (Ryan 2016).

However, if such grievances against police are longstanding, especially in certain Black communities, what explains the sporadic mobilization in response to certain incidents of police violence? As McAdam points out, "there is a constancy to grievances that seriously contradicts the causal significance assigned them" (McAdam 1982: 33). But McAdam further argues that discontent is *not* invariant and while objective conditions may be stable, the perceptions and subjective meanings attached to those conditions are variable (McAdam 1982: 33–34). Police violence, I argue, can serve as a focusing or "precipitating" event that makes discontent about anti-Black discrimination salient and meaningful.

This linkage of mobilization after a particular incident with police to the larger fight against anti-Black discrimination is important for understanding racial differences in who responds to officer-involved killings as well as for pinpointing the incidents that will generate a response. Even the Declaration of Independence suggests that any given incident is unlikely to spur action in isolation; that incident must be linked to "a long train of abuses." The killings of Black victims potentially can serve as "precipitating" incidents in ways that other killings cannot because of the belief, especially among Black people, that police are more likely to treat Black people unfairly.

The reality is that Black people are overrepresented among victims of officer-involved killings relative to their share of the population (Edwards, Esposito, and Lee 2018). Arnold notes that experiencing "Large and perceptible costs . . . are the principal stimuli" leading citizens to hold officials accountable (Arnold 1990: 51). Such threats have been shown to help citizens overcome barriers to participating in politics. To the extent that the prospect of unfair treatment of one's group by police can be threatening or anxiety-producing, it might make sense that people subjected to that threat might be motivated to participate in politics even more in order to alleviate it. The literature supports this point: individuals are more likely to join or donate to groups when told that policies that affect them are at stake (Hansen 1985; Miller and Krosnick 2004). Threat has been shown to mobilize groups especially when there are "associated steep costs of inaction," such as in the face of violence or deportation (Barreto et al. 2009: 747; White 2016).

Thus, to summarize briefly, public opinion research has shown that Black Americans are more likely than other racial groups to express discontent with police performance and to believe that police discriminate against Black people. These beliefs stem from negative personal and vicarious experiences with violence, harassment, unequal treatment, and poor service over the long term. This long-term discontent is made more salient over time by officer-involved killings that result from anti-Black discrimination. I argue that these killings are most likely to evoke a political response.

Of course, this argument begs the question: which killings are first, perceived and second, judged to be racially discriminatory? I argue that visibility and traceability are key to answering this question.

2.2 Race, Grievance, and Visibility

Attention to victims of officer-involved killings has exploded since Michael Brown was killed in Ferguson, Missouri in 2014. Since then, several social media accounts such as @BlackLivesMatter and @fatalencounters and other organizations have produced thousands of tweets and social media posts and collected hundreds of thousands of followers interested in news about victims of officer-involved killings (Tillery 2019). Responding to the public's appetite for such information, news organizations such as the Washington Post also started collecting data on the use of lethal force by police (2021c).

R. Douglas Arnold argues that policy effects must be perceptible in order to generate a citizen response (Arnold 1990: 48). Paul Pierson further refines this concept as visibility, or the idea that "voters must experience some discernible outcome that leads them to inquire about the cause of this outcome" (Pierson 1993). Arnold argues that "without perceptible effects there is nothing to activate the search process" that would lead a citizen to find a cause (Arnold 1990: 49). However, voters seeking to hold politicians accountable face information constraints and lack the knowledge they need to monitor government activity (Pierson 1993).

The use of force by police, even lethal force, often is imperceptible and thus particularly difficult for the public to assess. Neither police departments nor local governments willingly make information on officer-involved deaths readily available in most cases. The general consensus is that there are no reliable, consistent data on policing with respect to use of force, use of lethal force, complaints, or even *Terry* stops available over time and across the country. The data typically come from agency self-reports, FOIA requests, or more recently, attempts to collect data by news or nonpartisan organizations. As a result, most officer-involved deaths lack salience and are not known widely to the public despite the use of social media to publicize some incidents: fewer than half of victims of officer-involved deaths examined for this study trended on Google in their local area at the time of the killing.[3]

Several scholars argue that the informational deficits faced by the public can create incentives for politicians to manipulate the information available to voters in order to avoid blame for bad outcomes (Hacker and Pierson 2005; Pierson 1993; Weaver 1986). The evidence suggests that police and cities work actively to make their use of lethal force less visible to the public, as these theories suggest. For instance, in the case of Laquan McDonald, who was killed by Chicago police in 2015, paying McDonald's family millions of dollars for their silence and fighting the release of the dashcam video of his death was a way for the city to keep the story of McDonald's death from getting out (Harcourt 2015). Public officials also may obscure the use of force by blaming a medical condition. George Floyd was killed by Minneapolis police officer Derek Chauvin in May 2020 after Chauvin knelt on Mr. Floyd's neck for more than eight minutes. However, the initial statement released by the Minneapolis Police Department, titled "Man Dies after Medical Incident during Police Interaction," denied that officers injured Mr. Floyd and failed to mention that officers used any force against Mr. Floyd other than handcuffing him (Wade 2021). More generally, the failure to provide data or to investigate police use of force contributes to the lack of public visibility as well (2017a).

Despite these barriers to visibility, there are several ways that the public can become aware of deaths involving police operations. Arnold notes that the

[3] Victims' names were entered into Google Trends, along with the location of the killing. More detail will be provided in what follows.

media can increase visibility (Arnold 1990: 49), and news organizations do report on some police shootings or killings and have been doing so increasingly in recent years. Several news organizations, including the Washington Post, now maintain databases of officer-involved deaths. Also, as Section 4 will discuss, social justice organizations can help publicize officer-involved killings.

Proximity is another factor that increases visibility. Proximity can be thought of as an observer's closeness to an outcome, or how affected they are by an outcome. One definition, provided by Pierson, focuses on "whether those affected are part of a network" of other affected people (Pierson 1993: 622). Some people may learn about fatal incidents through social media, family, or community connections. To the extent that these experiences are shared among family, friends, and other interpersonal or organizational networks, the visibility of victims may be heightened, especially at the local level. However, when victims and their families lack extensive interpersonal connections, a killing still may not become known to the wider public.

Another definition of proximity, from Soss and Schram, focuses on whether incidents exist "as a tangible presence affecting people's lives in immediate, concrete ways versus existing as a distant object appraised for its effects elsewhere" (Soss and Schram 2007). Proximity may be geographic, temporal, or social (such as race, class, or gender) (Soss and Schram 2007). Experiencing negative effects of government actions "in immediate, concrete ways" is particularly effective for heightening attention and visibility (Soss and Schram 2007). Such disproportionate burdens heighten visibility (Mettler and Koch 2012). As noted previously, Black people are killed most disproportionately by the police (Edwards, Esposito, and Lee 2018), and such racial disproportionality in burdens has been shown to increase the visibility of government actions, especially among minority groups (Michener 2019; Rosenthal 2020). A similar dynamic may be at play among young people, who are killed disproportionately by police as well (Edwards, Esposito, and Lee 2018). Proximity also may play a role in the generational divide that has been observed among African Americans regarding police violence (Taylor 2016: 161).

Proximity may lead to information-seeking, thus heightening visibility. Uses and gratifications theory posits that individuals are active consumers of traditional and social media who seek out content that fulfills a wide variety of needs (Greene and Krcmar 2005; Kaye and Johnson 2002; Papacharissi and Rubin 2000). One such need, curiosity, is defined by Litman "as a desire to know, to see, or to experience that motivates exploratory behavior directed towards the acquisition of new information" (Litman 2005: 793). Information-seeking has long been a primary driver of television, print, and media consumption. Information-seeking satisfies curiosity caused by distress as well as interest

(Litman 2005). I argue that although officer-involved killings can generate attention, and thus visibility, through several pathways, proximity shapes whether that curiosity is caused by distress or mere interest.

Curiosity motivated by a desire to reduce distress, such as anxiety, uncertainty, or stress, can drive information-seeking (Litman 2005). In particular, when people are exposed to novel or threatening stimuli, they activate their surveillance systems (Coan et al. 2020; Ng and Zhao 2018; Semenza and Bernau 2020; Stroud 2017). Such surveillance systems allow individuals to monitor "the environment for threats and dangers" in order to protect themselves (Hoffner et al. 2009:198). Research has shown that attention to and information-seeking about morbid events, such as crimes, terrorist attacks, and disasters, are related to regulating feelings of uncertainty and anxiety (Boyle et al. 2004; Hoffner et al. 2009; Kubey and Peluso 1990).

Surveillance can lead to information-seeking about officer-involved killings because of fears about victimization. Seeking out information about incidents involving officer-involved killings can be driven not only by the high threat posed by a particular victim, *but also by the threat caused by the officer*. In this way, the racial disproportionality of officer-involved killings is important: this surveillance effect may lead Black and other observers to seek out information about police killings of unarmed Black victims because of a sense of threat or fear that something similar could happen to them or someone that they know (Appiah, Knobloch-Westerwick, and Alter 2013; Johnson and Kuhns 2009; Knobloch-Westerwick, Appiah, and Alter 2008). Similarly, a sense of linked fate, which ties individual well-being or success to the outcomes of the entire racial group (Dawson 1995), may lead to greater surveillance of officer-involved killings.

Attention to morbid events may also be caused by sympathy and concern for the welfare of victims, which may lead people to seek out information about how individuals involved in an incident fared (Hoffner et al. 2009). They may also look for reassurance of positive outcomes, such as healing, policy change, or justice (Goldenberg et al. 1999; Hoffner et al. 2009; Semenza and Bernau 2020). This aspect of curiosity may lead to information-seeking about low-threat victims of officer-involved killings, such as women and children, because "ideal victims in tragic incidents are innocent people who are believed to have no skills to defend themselves" (Zhang et al. 2019). The deaths of "children and other valued groups" are deeply mourned by the public, and child victims are more likely to generate public sympathy (McIvor 2012; Zhang et al. 2019). Women also are more interested in stories about crimes against other women for surveillance reasons (Aust and Zillmann 1996; Knobloch-Westerwick and Hastall 2006, 2010).

Of course, curiosity also may be motivated by enjoyment or interest, rather than a deficit of information (Litman 2005). Information-seeking can be driven by "anticipated pleasure from finding out information of a more casual, unessential, entertaining, or aesthetically pleasing nature, such as juicy gossip, an amusing anecdote, or an entertaining story" (Litman 2005: 799–800). Zuckerman and Litle find that "high sensation seekers" have greater interest "in presentations of violent or morbid and sexual events in the media and in live sports" because they increase "activity in central catecholamine systems" (Zuckerman and Litle 1986).

To summarize, scholars argue that visibility, or awareness of a government action, is an important precursor to mobilization. The literature suggests that not all victims of officer-involved killings are equally visible to all members of the public for a number of reasons. However, Black victims are more likely to be visible to Black people, especially young Black people, because this group is disproportionately affected by officer-involved killings. This greater proximity makes it more likely, because of surveillance and networks, that young Black people more than any other group will learn about and pay attention to officer-involved killings. Factors other than greater surveillance due to racial threat can affect visibility as well, however, because some people seek out information about officer-involved killings for reasons of empathy or entertainment.

2.3 The Traceability of Officer-Involved Killings

Grievances are "subjective, unstable, reactive, complicated, and incomplete" (Felstiner, Abel, and Sarat 1980: 637). Grievances are this way because they are socially constructed, as "individuals define and redefine their perceptions of experience and the nature of their grievances in response to the communications, behavior, and expectations of a range of people" (Felstiner, Abel, and Sarat 1980: 638). Almost all grievances can be viewed from a variety of perspectives. This subjectivity of grievances, I argue, makes them particularly susceptible to framing effects.

Framing effects occur "when (often small) changes in the presentation of an issue or an event produce (sometimes large) changes of opinion" (Chong and Druckman 2007: 104). Different frames place emphasis on alternate facts or make new circumstances relevant or salient in ways that can alter public opinion. When an opinion is strongly held, presenting new frames may not alter the opinion formulated after presentation with the initial frame (Matthes and Schemer 2012).

Traceability is the ability of citizens to "link [an] outcome to some government action" (Pierson 1993). Traceability, like visibility, is malleable

(Arnold 1990; Hacker and Pierson 2005; Pierson 1993). As Arnold writes, "Traceability is a subjective process that depends on what citizens believe about cause and effect" (Arnold, 1990: 48). Framing is important to these beliefs about cause and effect, especially for audiences who are more distant from an event (Soss and Schram 2007).

I argue that political mobilization will occur in response to incidents that can be traced to anti-Black discrimination. However, only certain incidents plausibly can be framed as the result of anti-Black discrimination. A key component of the traceability of an action or policy involves its complexity: actions with long causal chains or multiple "stages or uncertainties" are less traceable to specific government actions (Pierson 1993). I argue that incidents characterized by the intentional use of force without a legally relevant justification have the greatest potential to be framed in terms of anti-Black discrimination. Deaths where force was not clearly intentional, or that may have been motivated by legally relevant factors such as bystander or officer safety, have more complicated causal chains and are less likely to be framed in terms of anti-Black discrimination.

2.3.1 Was There an Intentional Use of Lethal Force?

The use of lethal force might seem obvious, given the fact that a person died in an officer-involved killing. In a typical year, about three-quarters of officer-involved killings involve lethal force such as a gunshot. These injuries are typically clearly the result of police action, although occasionally in situations involving multiple shooters there may be some doubt as to who fired the fatal shot.

However, there are many circumstances in which people die during an encounter with an officer where lethal force was not used. These causal chains often are complex because they involve multiple factors. Research shows that using tasers or restraints on people under the influence of drugs or in medical distress can exacerbate medical distress or even cause death, such that many departments restrict the use of force on people in crisis (1995; Pasquier et al. 2011; 2017a). However, official reports may attribute those deaths to the medical issues while ignoring or minimizing the contribution of the restraint or shock to the death (White et al. 2013). The most troubling case of this phenomenon involves excited delirium, which is a controversial medical condition "associated with severe agitation, and autonomic arousal" usually brought about because of mental illness or drug use (O'Brien and Thom 2014). Excited delirium has been blamed for sudden deaths in custody, but often subjects whose deaths are attributed to excited delirium also were restrained, tased, or asphyxiated with choke holds or knees to the neck (O'Brien and Thom 2014; Truscott 2008). Other suspects may die of heart attacks, drug overdoses, or other medical conditions while in custody.

Car accidents are another frequent cause of officer-involved deaths. These accidents can occur when a suspect or officer hits a pedestrian or other driver during a chase, an officer hits a suspect during a chase, or an officer hits a pedestrian or other suspect outside of a police chase scenario. In some cases, suspects who hit bystanders or kill their passengers while fleeing police are charged with murder; see (2017b) for an example. On other occasions, officers may be prosecuted and cities may pay damages when people die in officer-involved automobile accidents, especially in cases where the officer violated department policies or laws. In 2016, the families of several victims ultimately received settlements as a result of vehicle accidents, such as in the deaths of Marilyn Bettencourt of Stockton, California and Dorothy Smith Wright of Atlanta, Georgia.

Research shows that the manner of death does matter for evaluating the use of lethal force; the public responds differently to intentional uses of lethal force than to other causes of death. Pica et al. find that experimental subjects evaluate officers who kill suspects more negatively when they use a gun rather than a less-lethal taser or assault gloves (Pica et al. 2020). Streeter also finds that people killed with guns are more likely to be protested (Streeter 2019: 103). Most victims of officer-involved killings are shot by police.

2.3.2 Was There a Legally Relevant Justification for the Use of Force?

Blame is an essential component of a grievance. According to Arnold, an officer-involved killing must be *identifiable* as the result of a government action – people respond with protest or approval only when they hold the government responsible for an action or policy in some way (Arnold 1990). Identifiable government actions must be causally linked to the outcome a person observes (Arnold 1990: 48); therefore, it matters whether the officer's actions or the victim's actions were thought to have caused the use of lethal force.

The current legal regime, ushered in by the US Supreme Court in *Tennessee* v. *Garner* (1985), dictates that the most important factor in whether the use of deadly force is justified is the dangerousness of the suspect or victim. In *Garner*, the Supreme Court found that an officer shooting a person to defend themselves or another person from imminent danger is a legitimate use of lethal force, but that lethal force also may be used to prevent escape when "the officer has probable cause to believe that the suspect poses a significant threat of death or serious physical injury to the officer or others." However, the Court clearly stated, "A police officer may not seize an unarmed, nondangerous suspect by shooting him dead" (*Tennessee* v. *Garner* 1985).

The Supreme Court further refined the use of force in *Graham* v. *Conor* (1989). In *Graham*, the Court articulated a three-prong test for evaluating whether police used appropriate force on a suspect. First, it is important to consider the "severity of the crime at issue," second, "whether the suspect poses an immediate threat to the safety of the officers or others," and third, "whether he is actively resisting arrest or attempting to evade arrest by flight." The Court also found that the "'reasonableness' of a particular use of force must be judged from the perspective of a reasonable officer on the scene, rather than with the 20/20 vision of hindsight."

Victim dangerousness also is important to judgments of officer-involved deaths at the state level; however, states vary in their standards for assessing victim dangerousness. Prior to the Court's decision in *Garner*, state and local laws governing police use of deadly force fell into four categories: "The Anti-Felony Rule; The Defense-of-Life Rule; the Model Penal Code; and The Forcible Felony Rule" (Tennenbaum 1994: 242). The anti-felony rule, from English common law, granted officers the right to use any means or any force necessary to arrest felony suspects or prevent them from fleeing (Tennenbaum 1994). This meant that officers could even shoot and kill unarmed fleeing suspects. The Tennessee statute at issue in *Garner*, as cited by the Court, read "[i]f, after notice of the intention to arrest the defendant, he either flee or forcibly resist, the officer may use all the necessary means to effect the arrest." In contrast, the defense-of-life rule limits acceptable uses of deadly force to situations in which it is necessary to protect either the officer's own life or that of a civilian on the scene (Tennenbaum 1994). The forcible felony rule is an intermediate standard that allows police to use deadly force when apprehending people suspected of committing certain dangerous felonies such as rape, murder, or armed robbery (Tennenbaum 1994).

The standard adopted in *Garner* closely follows the Model Penal Code recommendation, which limits the use of lethal force to two conditions: first, when the crime involved the use of deadly force, and second, there is a "substantial risk that the suspect will cause death or serious bodily harm if his apprehension is delayed." After the Court adopted this standard for cases arising under Section 1983, many states changed their own rules; the Court found that twenty-three states had the anti-felony standard in statutes or by case law in 1985 when *Garner* was decided, and that number had declined to twelve states that still retained that standard by 2015 (Flanders and Welling 2015).

2.3.3 Factors Affecting Public Judgments about Justification

Although legal standards for justification exist at the federal level and in the states, it is not clear that the public uses them to evaluate officers' use of force. Meares, Tyler, and Gardner find that the lawfulness or constitutionality of police actions has little to do with how the public evaluates them (Meares, Tyler, and Gardener 2015). A significant proportion of the public seems to evaluate dangerousness differently than the Supreme Court standard. Moreover, victim, incident, and observer characteristics also matter for public attributions of blame for officer-involved killings.

With respect to victim behavior, there are segments of the public who are both more and less strict than the Supreme Court. Cullen et al. (1996) find that 15 to 20 percent of respondents would approve of police using deadly force to stop a person fleeing after stealing a purse, jewelry, or a car, and 40 percent would approve of using deadly force to stop a suspect fleeing after selling drugs or burglarizing a house (a scenario the Court explicitly deemed unacceptable in *Garner*). On the other end of the scale, some people do not accept the use of deadly force in situations the court would permit: 16 percent of respondents would not approve of using deadly force to stop a fleeing armed robber, and 10 percent would not approve of using deadly force to stop a fleeing rapist (Cullen et al. 1996). This discrepancy between law and public standards goes beyond just the use of lethal force. In fact, a substantial and growing part of the public disapproves of police violence under any circumstances, even nonlethal force. Mourtgos and Adams find that 34 percent of General Social Survey (GSS) respondents in 2018 answered "no" when asked, "Are there any situations you can imagine in which you would approve of a policeman striking an adult male citizen?" (Mourtgos and Adams 2020). The number of people saying "no" has increased since 1973, when 23 percent said there were no situations in which they would approve (Mourtgos and Adams 2020). Thirty-five percent of 2018 GSS respondents said they would not approve of an officer striking a suspect who was "attempting to escape custody" and 15 percent said they would not approve of police striking a suspect who was "attacking the policeman" (Mourtgos and Adams 2020). Streeter finds evidence that victim behavior matters: unarmed victims are more likely to be protested and people who shoot at the police are less likely to be protested than the baseline (Streeter 2019).

Public opinion about police use of force, like most aspects of policing, is shaped by race. Several studies show that Black people are less comfortable with police use of force than are White people (Cullen et al. 1996; Jefferis, Butcher, and Hanley 2011; Johnson and Kuhns 2009; Mourtgos and Adams 2020). This distinction may be attributable to differences across racial groups in social dominance orientation, right-wing authoritarianism, and blind patriotism (Perkins and Bourgeois 2006). Racial differences in the perceptions of the fairness of the criminal justice system may matter as well (Peffley and Hurwitz 2010).

Incident characteristics also affect attributions of blame to the extent that they affect the certainty or clarity with which observers can judge use of lethal force. For instance, the presence of recordings of the incident may make a difference. Experiments conducted by Mullinix, Bolsen, and Norris show that exposure to videos depicting controversial uses of lethal and nonlethal force produced large, statistically significant increases in anger, upset, and anxiety, and for this set of emotional responses, the videos produced greater effects than just the text alone (Mullinix, Bolsen, and Norris 2020). Video viewers also were more likely to pursue political remedies for injustice (Glasford 2013). Streeter also finds that public videos increase the likelihood of protest (Streeter 2019: 103).

The effects of videos are unstable and depend on such factors as observer beliefs and characteristics as well as framing. Testa and Dietrich (2017) find that telling respondents that the video they were shown was released to confirm a charge of police misconduct led them to see the police stop as less legitimate, viewed the officer's behavior as more negative, and thought race was more likely to play a role in shaping the interaction (Testa and Dietrich 2017: 16). Culhane, Boman and Schweitzer (2016) got different results in the same experiment conducted before and after Michael Brown was killed in Ferguson, Missouri in 2014. In the study conducted prior to Brown's death, video evidence tended to make mock jurors more certain that a killing was justified; after Brown's death, the same video evidence tended to make jurors less certain about the justification of a use of deadly force (Culhane, Boman, and Schweitzer 2016). Studies also show that the perspective of the video, such as whether it is from a body camera or other source, shapes its effects on viewers (Birck 2018). Cognitive biases based on preexisting racial stereotypes or evaluations of police also shape viewers' interpretations of recordings of incidents (Kahan, Hoffman, and Braman 2009).

Finally, victim characteristics affect conceptions of blameworthiness. The Supreme Court focuses on dangerousness as a key factor in whether the use of force by officers is justified, but acknowledges in *Garner* "the practical difficulties of attempting to assess the suspect's dangerousness." Assessing dangerousness is difficult because conceptions of dangerousness are related to stereotypes about race, gender, and other characteristics. Such stereotypes about victims can influence whether people interpret police actions in a given case as just or unjust (Peffley and Hurwitz 2010; Perkins and Bourgeois 2006).

Race is key to evaluations about the justice of an officer-involved killing. Early research has shown that African-American suspects are perceived as more dangerous than White suspects, and racial stereotypes about Black people affect how White observers view police use of force (Dukes and Gaither 2017). African-American deaths also generate less sympathy on social media (Zhang et al. 2019). However, recent research also has shown that campaigns by Black Lives Matter have moved the public to view officer-involved killings of Black victims with greater suspicion. Research subjects are more likely to view officer-involved killings of Black victims as unjustified, and officers were believed to be more guilty of errors when they shot Black victims (Huff, Alvarez, and Miller 2018; Pica et al. 2020). Streeter finds that victim race is strongly related to protest rates; Black victims are more likely to be protested than White or Latino victims (Streeter 2019). Other factors, such as gender, also affect perceptions of victim dangerousness (Hollander 2001).

2.3.4 Traceability to Racial Discrimination

I argue that mobilization in response to officer-involved killings will be more likely when Black observers are responding to Black victims. The literature supports the idea that Black grievances, stemming from personal or vicarious negative experiences with police, are important for Black evaluations of police–citizen interactions (Braga et al. 2014; Peffley and Hurwitz 2010; Tuch and Weitzer 1997). These grievances also are linked to racial discrimination: predispositions about system fairness are particularly salient to Black evaluations of interactions that involve Black citizens (Hurwitz and Peffley 2005). Peffley, Hurwitz, and Mondak find that Black and Latino survey respondents are more likely than White respondents to attribute racial disparities in criminal justice outcomes to racial discrimination against Black people rather than criminal or aggressive behavior (Peffley, Hurwitz, and Mondak 2017). Similarly, specific incidents of police brutality involving Rodney King and Malice Green were more likely to increase attributions of racial discrimination among Black respondents than White respondents (Sigelman et al. 1997). Williamson, Einstein, and Trump's discovery that Black Lives Matter solidarity protests against police violence are more likely to occur in places that had an officer-involved killing of a Black person in the past provides further evidence that mobilization depends on connecting officer-involved killings to other victims in a broader movement rather than just responding to them individually (Williamson, Trump, and Einstein 2018).

However, I also argue that the presence of a legally relevant explanation for officer-involved killings will moderate this mobilization by making it more difficult to attribute a killing to anti-Black discrimination. Black Americans are not always opposed to the police use of force, particularly against aggressive people. According to the 2016 GSS, 71 percent of Black respondents said that it was appropriate for police to use force against a citizen attacking police with their fists.[4] The same attention to victim dangerousness is at play among Black observers, admittedly not to the same degree as among observers of other races.

Victim dangerousness may moderate the mobilization against officer-involved killings by affecting perceived threat. Respectability politics refers to a strategy of Black uplift in which "'proper' and 'respectable' behavior" was used to prove "Blacks worthy of equal civil and political rights" (Higginbotham 1992: 271). Respectability politics assumes "that if Blacks assimilate and behave more like Whites, equal treatment will follow" (Bunyasi and Smith 2019: 185). This idea links perceptions of threat to victim dangerousness: since "nonconformity was equated with deviance and pathology, and was often cited as a cause of racial inequality and injustice," people who conform to notions of proper behavior might not feel that police will treat them the same as a person who does not (Higginbotham 1992: 271).

This dynamic plays out clearly in public discussions of officer-involved killings. For instance, activists attribute the muted response to the death of Ma'Khia Bryant, a sixteen-year-old who was shot by Columbus, Ohio police in the spring of 2021, to the fact that she was not a "perfect victim" (Cineas 2021). Indeed, several prominent figures came out to defend the officer's actions. Representative Val Demmings, a former police chief, said, "Everybody has the benefit of slowing the video down and seizing the perfect moment. The officer on the street does not have that ability. He or she has to make those split-second decisions, and they're tough" (Cineas 2021). DJ Envy also defended the police officer on *The Breakfast Club*, a popular radio show, "I mean, the cop got a call that said that, you know, these women were jumping somebody. They hop out the car and see a woman going at another woman with a knife. Yeah, maybe, if they would have shot her in the foot, or shot her in the leg, who's to say she still couldn't stab the young girl" (2021b). Even in the face of Charlamagne tha God's arguments about racial discrimination in the use of force by police, Envy did not think that racial discrimination mattered to the outcome in this case. In fact, Envy and others stressed the officer's duty to defend the other person in the fight, who also was Black.

The fact that some Black observers share this thinner conception of racial discrimination, that it only operates in the absence of dangerous behavior by the victim, does not mean that everyone does. There is ample evidence that many

[4] Analysis generated using the GSS Data Explorer (https://gssdataexplorer.norc.org).

people support a more capacious conception of racial discrimination (Ransby 2018). For instance, Cineas writes:

> Bryant's death has become a debate that questions a child's actions – and worthiness to live – instead of another example of the racism of policing and the institution's failure to provide wholesome support, care, and safety for the communities it serves. The insistence that Reardon had no other option than to take Bryant's life to save others – though he risked everyone's life in the process – displays the lack of consideration and value that society places on the lives of Black girls and women. (Cineas 2021)

This conception sees racial differences in treatment even among dangerous suspects, contrasting the treatment of people like Bryant with that given to White mass shooters:

> There are countless examples of police peacefully apprehending White boys and men wielding weapons. Just last year police officers in Kenosha, Wisconsin, handed water bottles to and thanked 17-year-old Kyle Rittenhouse, a self-described militia member who carried an AR-15-style rifle during the unrest that followed the police shooting of Jacob Blake. Rittenhouse was allowed to leave the scene after fatally shooting two people and harming another, though the police had been informed that he was the shooter. (Cineas 2021)

Threadcraft observes that some activists go even further, challenging "the state's assertion that thug should mark the line between he who lives and he who must die" (Threadcraft 2017: 560). People who share this thicker conception of racial discrimination still may mobilize when lethal force is used against dangerous suspects; however, I argue that mobilization is less likely for suspects who are considered dangerous.

2.4 Conclusion

In this section, I assert the importance of grievances for understanding mobilization in response to officer-involved killings. Specifically, I argue that attention and mobilization around officer-involved killings can only be understood in light of concerns about anti-Black discrimination. I argue that people concerned about anti-Black discrimination will pay more attention to officer-involved killings and mobilize in response to those that they can attribute to such racism. Thus, we should expect that race will be an important explanatory factor in the politics of officer-involved killings. First, because young Black people are most burdened and most proximate to officer-involved killings, they should be most likely to pay attention to and mobilize when they occur. Second, the racial disproportionality in killings also suggests that only killings of Black victims should consistently mobilize a public response. Finally, only those killings that are attributable to racial discrimination, but not other legally relevant factors such as victim behavior, should motivate a political response. Taken together, I expect mobilization to follow a particular pattern: killings of low-threat Black victims will serve as precipitating events that will mobilize young Black people concerned about anti-Black racism. I explore this hypothesis further in the next section.

3 A Closer Look at Mobilization in the Aftermath of Officer-Involved Killings

In this section, I present data on mobilization in response to officer-involved killings to test my claims about the central importance of grievances as an explanatory factor. As the previous section theorizes, mobilization in response to officer-involved killings primarily is driven by concerns about anti-Black discrimination. The extent to which deaths focus attention on such racial discrimination will predict who mobilizes after an officer-involved killing and when.

The analysis uses two sets of data to explore mobilization in response to officer-involved killings. First, I examine data on individual victims of officer-involved killings to see who is most likely to generate public attention and protest. Second, I present analyses from other articles in this research project in order to see how exposure to victims of officer-involved killings affects political attitudes and participation among observers.

These analyses send a clear and consistent message: race is key to understanding and predicting mobilization in the aftermath of an officer-involved killing. Race affects both *who* mobilizes as well as *what* mobilizes. Among victims of officer-involved killings, Black victims are by far the most likely to get public attention and to get protested. Among observers, exposure only to Black victims of officer-involved killings consistently affects political attitudes and behavior, and only among young Black observers. Across all the analyses, officer and victim behavior moderate the effect of race: whether of victims or observers, mobilization is most likely when force is used without a legally relevant rationale, suggesting that concerns about discrimination are at the forefront.

The discussion that follows will focus heavily on the victim-level analysis, presenting the data as well as an overview of officer-involved killings that took place in one year, 2016.[5] Because the observer-level data appear in other

[5] I chose 2016 as the baseline year for the analysis primarily because nationwide survey data such as the Collaborative Multiracial Political Survey, which I use in this project to measure individual participation, are available only in federal election years. I wanted all the analyses to be based in the same year. However, it is worth noting that the observer-level analysis considers deaths that happened over a wider time period (late 2016 to early 2018) due to the research design. Some

publications, the discussion of those results will be briefer. Much of the technical discussion of the methods is available in those articles as well as in the online appendix to this Element.

3.1 Data

Both the victim- and observer-level analyses rely on data from FatalEncounters.org, a website that collects and then researches media- and crowd-sourced information on officer-involved killings. Fatal Encounters data are preferable to data from government sources because data from government sources (such as the FBI's Supplemental Homicide Reports) do not present a full and accurate portrait of officer-involved killings across the United States. According to Legewie and Fagan, counts of officer-involved killings based on the Supplemental Homicide Reports are off by nearly 40 percent because the reports are missing data for 19.5 percent of cities and because many cities who do report data underreport the number of incidents by nearly 30 percent (Legewie and Fagan 2016: 15). Legewie and Fagan find that the Fatal Encounters data missed only 3 percent of the cases that fit their definition of officer-involved killings, a significant improvement over the federal data (Legewie and Fagan 2016). In the years they analyzed, Legewie and Fagan excluded 17 percent of fatalencounters.org data because they did not fit their definition of officer-involved killings (Legewie and Fagan 2016). Similarly, the analysis presented here, which looks at different years, excludes the 15 percent of incidents that fatalencounters.org attributes to suicides.

As Section 2 describes, the level of culpability assigned to the victim and the officer also may be related to mobilization. Fatal Encounters did not include indicators of victim dangerousness, and such determinations are very complicated. An observer might use many factors to determine whether they think officers were justified in using lethal force in a particular incident, including victim race and gender or criminal history. This study relies on just two dimensions to assign culpability: whether the victim was posing a serious threat to the safety of officers or bystanders when their death occurred, and whether officers followed proper procedures during the encounter. Videos, news, and official reports were used to code victim behavior into three categories: (1) if the

people may argue that general election years are special and may produce effects that are not generalizable to other years. I would argue, however, that the number of fatal police shootings in each year is relatively similar between 2015 and 2017 (N = 995, 958, 983 respectively), as is the number of officer-involved deaths overall between 2014 and 2017 (N = 1714, 1611, 1599, 1767) (Fatal Encounters 2023; The Washington Post 2023). Moreover, choosing a year to conduct a national analysis that is not an election year somewhere is nearly impossible, given the fact that many states and cities elect their leaders in odd-numbered years and those elections may be even more sensitive to the effects of a particular incident.

victim was clearly not posing a threat to officers or others at the time of death, and (3) if the victim was posing a clear threat (and the officer followed proper procedures). The middle category, (2), is reserved for instances in which the victim may have engaged in some type of threatening behavior but officers may have made a mistake or acted outside of protocol. Another way of considering this coding, from the perspective of the officers' behavior, is that in categories 1 and 2, the officer bears all or at least some responsibility for the death of the victim. More detail on the coding is provided in the online appendix.

I use Google Trends to measure the visibility of particular victims of officer-involved killings. Several papers have used Google Trends data as a measure of public attention to particular phenomena (Lee, Kim, and Scheufele 2016; Semenza and Bernau 2020). This service "analyzes a percentage of Google web searches to determine how many searches were done over a certain period of time."[6] For any search term entered, Google Trends returns a number from zero to 100 that indicates the popularity of that search term relative to others within a certain location and time period. Google Trends filters out terms that few people are searching, such that "search terms with low volume appear as 0 for a given time period" or as having not enough data. For this project, each victim's name and location were entered into Google Trends to get the city and national scores. Incidents count as "trending" if the city-level or national-level score was higher than thirty.[7] An incident did not have to be the most searched agenda item in an area in order to count as trending; the measure was designed to identify victims who generated even a moderate level of interest.

3.2 Victim Level Analysis

The primary analysis conducted for this Element explores which victims generated public attention and protest after their deaths. For this analysis, I consider only victims from the Fatal Encounters data who were killed in 2016. There were 1,587 people who died in officer-involved killings that year (as of when I downloaded the database). However, similar to Legewie and Fagan, the analysis presented here excludes 248 incidents that were ruled suicides

[6] https://storage.googleapis.com/gweb-news-initiative-training.appspot.com/upload/GO802_NewsInitiativeLessons_Fundamentals-L04-GoogleTrends_1saYVCP.pdf

[7] While thirty is an arbitrary choice, it is worth noting that for national and city-level interest, more than 90 percent of the 1284 victims killed in 2016 had peak interest scores of either zero or 100. For national interest, only fourteen victims scored between one and fifty; at the city level, only fourteeen victims scored between zero and ninety-nine. Only three victims had scores on either scale between one and thirty. In other words, very few victims would be reclassified if the cutoff were changed.

(15.8 percent). Three cases involved officers only peripherally.[8] An additional twenty-two incidents where the victim's name was missing or withheld and twenty-seven incidents in which an incident could not be matched to a valid census place code also were excluded from the data. The final sample size is 1,284 victims.

Fatal Encounters includes information about the victim and the incident that may affect whether a person is protested. The victim's age in years is included in the models (age squared was not statistically significant and thus excluded from the final models presented here). The victim's race was imputed in the original dataset and was included in the models through indicators for Black, Latino, Asian, and Native American with White as the reference category (this category also includes the one Arab/Middle Easterner as White, following the US Census). An indicator for female was included, with male (and one transgender person whose preferred gender was unknown) as the reference category. Indicators for gunshot and vehicle accidents as causes of death were included in the models, with all other causes (bludgeoning, asphyxiation, tasers, falls, etc.) forming the reference categories.

I and my coders researched all 1,284 victims individually in order to add several variables to the data. We searched television and print media, social media sites, YouTube, court records, and government reports to add data on the availability of audio and video recordings by hand.[9] We also coded the dependent variable, an indicator for whether a victim's death was protested, by searching Google, news reports, and social media for the victim's name and location of death. Additionally, archives of three newspapers in each state were searched for protest events for particular victims of officer-involved killings for all of 2016 in in addition to searches for public records, court filings, print and television news articles, and social media posts through Google and other media.

An event was characterized as a protest if the incident included any message decrying the death of the particular person, calling for further investigation or government action on the case, or denouncing police violence more broadly. Protests did not include only planned marches or demonstrations, and could be of any size. Thus, the events are wide-ranging and include everything from riots to group takeovers of city meetings, to prayer vigils-turned-marches, and even

[8] One of these cases involved a drug overdose; the other two victims were shot by their mother, who was then killed by police herself.

[9] Recordings came from a number of sources, including officer dashboard and body cameras, surveillance cameras, 911 recordings, and cell phone video. Incidents were coded as "1" if there was any mention of a full or partial audio or video recording that captured the use of lethal force. If there is no recording, or only a recording that did not capture the use of force, the indicator was coded "0."

to just a few family members standing around with signs. Several families held vigils for victims that did not contain a message aimed at police or government; these vigils did not count as protests for these purposes. Protests could take place at any point after a person's death, and many protests took place in the aftermath of prosecutorial decisions or court rulings, on the anniversary of the victim's birth or death, or in conjunction with other deaths in the area. Some victims killed in 2016 were not protested for the first time until after the death of George Floyd in 2020; these protests were not counted in the data. Many protests were staged in honor of multiple victims; in these cases, each victim was coded as having a protest. In one incident, officers themselves protested at court because one of their fellow officers was charged for killing a person in the data; this incident was not counted as a protest of a victim's death.

This measure of protest is perhaps both over- and under-inclusive. It includes any event designed to convey disagreement with the police action, no matter how small. However, this coding scheme may miss many protests that are too small to get mentioned in the news or social media (Earl et al. 2004).

Finally, contextual data were attached to account for organizational capacity and political opportunity structure. These data include place-level percent of residents in poverty and the proportion of residents who are Black or Latino in 2016 from the US Census Bureau; the place-level presence of social justice organizations per capita from the 2016 IRS Master List of Exempt organizations; and counts of unique scandals involving law enforcement collected by the National Police Misconduct Reporting Project of the CATO Institute.[10] As an additional measure of misconduct, an indicator of whether the local police department was under investigation by the US Department of Justice in 2016 also was included.

3.2.1 Overview of Officer-involved Killings in 2016

Because the facts surrounding many officer-involved killings are relatively unknown, it makes sense to spend time describing the data in detail. There are 1,284 victims remaining in the data after cleaning and coding the data as described previously. As Table 1 shows, the victims are disproportionately Black: Black people make up only 13.4 percent of the US population, but were 29.0 percent of officer-involved killings in 2016. Similarly, non-Hispanic White

[10] Now www.unlawfulshield.com. Since 2009, the organization has tweeted more than 27,000 news alerts of police misconduct from across the nation ranging from excessive use of force, to corruption, to criminal behavior. Researchers vetted, categorized, and updated the misconduct claims regularly. While news accounts of police misconduct do not represent an accurate measure of all misconduct that takes place, it does help give a sense of scandals and misconduct that are visible to the general public. The 2016 file was used for this analysis.

Table 1 Descriptive statistics

	Min	*Median*	*Mean*	*Std. Dev.*	*Max*	*N*
Trended	0	0	0.45	0.50	1	1284
Protested	0.00	0.00	0.08	0.28	1.00	1284
Low-Threat	0.00	0.00	0.43	0.50	1.00	1284
Recording	0.00	0.00	0.35	0.48	1.00	1284
Age	0.33	34.00	36.32	14.05	87.00	1272
Black Victim	0.00	0.00	0.29	0.45	1.00	1284
Latino Victim	0.00	0.00	0.16	0.36	1.00	1284
Native American Victim	0.00	0.00	0.02	0.15	1.00	1284
Asian Victim	0.00	0.00	0.02	0.14	1.00	1284
Female Victim	0.00	0.00	0.08	0.28	1.00	1284
Gunshot	0.00	1.00	0.77	0.42	1.00	1284
Auto Accident	0.00	0.00	0.16	0.36	1.00	1284
Federal Investigation	0.00	0.00	0.04	0.19	1.00	1284
Percent in Poverty	0.00	18.90	19.10	8.32	63.60	1284
Proportion Black	0.00	0.07	0.16	0.19	0.95	1284
Proportion Latino	0.00	0.13	0.20	0.20	0.98	1284
Social Justice Orgs Per Capita	0	0	0.00003	0.00006	0.00090	1284
Misconduct Incidents Per Capita	0	0	0.00001	0.00002	0.00038	1284

Americans are underrepresented relative to their share of the US population in these data: White people were 60.1 percent of the US population but only 50.4 percent of officer-involved killings in 2016. Other groups were only slightly misrepresented relative to their population share; Asian and Pacific Islanders were 1.9 percent, Native American and Alaskan Natives were 2.3 percent, and Latinos were 15.7 percent of the victims.

Victims also were disproportionately young. The median age of the sample was 34. However, Black and Latino victims were younger overall: the median age of Black victims was the lowest at 29.5, while the median ages for Latino and Native American victims were 31.0 and 31.5, respectively. White and Asian victims were slightly older; the median age for these groups was 38.0 and 36.0, respectively.

Women were underrepresented among the victims of officer-involved killings, and the circumstances surrounding the deaths of the small subset of female victims are distinctly different from those of the men. Only 107 (8.2 percent of the sample) victims were female, 73.6 percent of whom were coded as low-threat. Fifty-two percent of female victims were killed in car accidents. Several women were victims of off-duty violence. For instance, Joyce Quayweay, Greta Kurian, and Nikki Bascomb were killed by their intimate partners, who were police officers. Another victim, Kaylee Sawyer, was kidnapped and murdered by a campus safety officer.

With respect to victim threat overall, 554 (43.1 percent) victims were coded as low or moderate threat. The level of threat varies by race: Black victims were more likely to be coded as low-threat: 185 (50.3 percent) Black victims were coded low-threat compared with 260 (40.2 percent) White victims, 79 (39.3 percent) Latino victims, 11 (44.0 percent) Asian victims, and 11 (37.9 percent) Native American victims. There were 730 high-threat victims in the data.

The incidents also vary with respect to several other factors that may be important to traceability. An audio or video recording of information relevant to the use of lethal force was available in 35.4 percent of incidents. An overwhelming number (77.1 percent) of victims died from gunshot wounds, while 15.6 percent died in motor vehicle accidents. Manner of death varies by threat level: 27.8 percent of low-threat victims died in motor vehicle accidents, compared with only 6.4 percent of high-threat victims.

Although officer-involved killings seem to be in the news all the time, less than half of all victims of officer-involved killings spark public attention. Only 44.9 percent (576) of the victims of officer-involved killings in this sample trended on Google locally or nationally. As Figure 1 shows, race was an important factor: Black victims were more likely to trend on Google (51.3 percent) than White or Latino victims (40.8 percent and 44.2 percent, respectively). Native American and Asian victims were most likely to trend on Google at 55.1 percent and 60.0 percent, respectively, though their overall numbers were much lower than the other groups and may be statistically unreliable as a result. Manner of death also distinguished victims who trended from those who did not: 48.8 percent of victims killed by gunshots trended on Google, compared with 31.6 percent of victims who died by other means. Victim threat level did not seem to matter to the level of public attention, as Figure 2 highlights: 45.3 percent of low-threat victims trended on Google, while 44.5 percent of high-threat victims did so.

It may be surprising, given the visibility of protest in media and public discourse, that only 106 of the victims of officer-involved killings in 2016 had their deaths protested (8.3 percent). Of course, that year, some high-profile

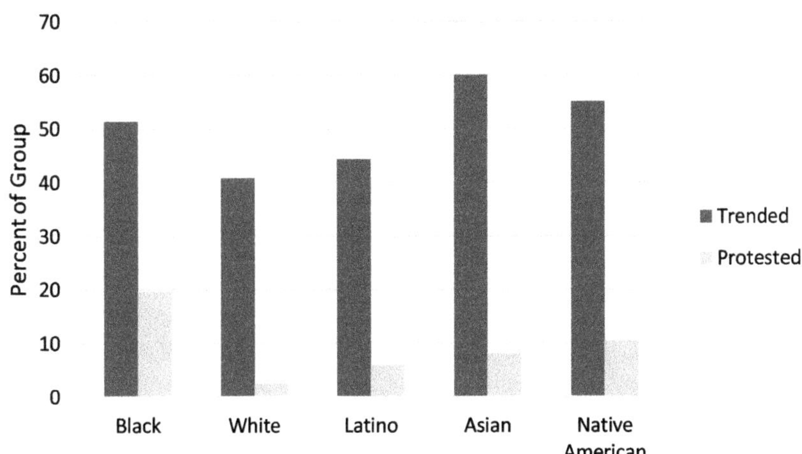

Figure 1 Public attention and protest, by race of victim

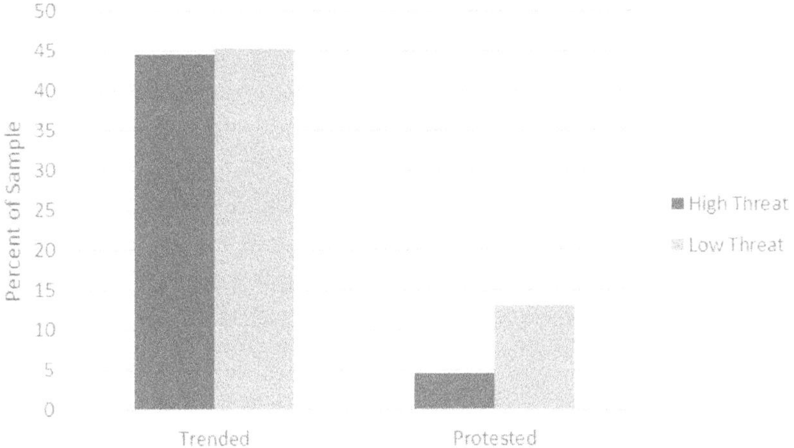

Figure 2 Public attention and protest, by victim threat level

deaths led to multiple protests – Alton Sterling, Philando Castile, Korryn Gaines, Keith Scott, and Edgar Camacho-Alvarado are among the dead. However, the high level of protest activity seems to be concentrated on relatively few victims. What factors differentiate the protested victims from the ones who were not?

At first glance, race clearly shapes the likelihood that a victim's death is protested. Seventy-three of the 106 protested deaths (68.9 percent) involved

Black victims, and Black victims' deaths are protested at a much higher rate than other groups. As shown in Figure 1, 19.6 percent of Black victims's deaths were protested, compared with 2.5 percent of White, 6.0 percent of Latino, 10.3 percent of Native American, and 8.0 percent of Asian deaths.

The traceability of the government's role also seems to matter to whether someone's death is protested. As the literature on the divergence between legal and popular definitions of the acceptable uses of lethal force might lead us to expect, there are a few protests of deaths involving high-threat victims. However, as Figure 2 shows, only 4.5 percent of deaths involving high-threat victims were protested, compared with 13.2 percent of deaths of low-threat victims. This low rate of protest even among low-threat victims is surprising: most officer-involved killings are not protested, even among the 554 victims who posed only a low or moderate threat to officers. Nearly all, 94.3 percent, of people whose deaths were protested were killed with a gun; overall, 10.1 percent of people killed with a gun had their deaths protested, compared with 2.0 percent of people killed by vehicle, taser, or other means, suggesting that intentional uses of force are more likely to be traced to government action, as expected.

The data presented in the previous section showed that victim threat level varied by race. Looking more closely at which deaths were protested, it is clear that these two factors matter tremendously for protest. Of the 106 people in the sample whose deaths were protested, 44.3 percent were low-threat Black victims. Low-threat Black victims generated the highest rate of protest at 25.1 percent; however, it is important to note that almost three-quarters of the deaths of even this group were not protested. More surprisingly, 24.5 percent of deaths that were protested were of high-threat Black victims. In fact, high-threat Black victims were more likely to generate protest than even low-threat White victims. For instance, there were twenty-six deaths of high-threat Black victims protested (14.1 percent protest rate), compared with only thirteen deaths of low-threat White victims (5.0 percent protest rate).

3.2.2 Multivariate Analysis: Methods

The bivariate analysis shows the importance of race and threat level for both public attention and protest of officer-involved killings. However, these associations may be spurious, so multivariate analyses are necessary to account for potentially confounding factors. Because the dependent variables are dichotomous, it is necessary to deploy logit regression. Due to the complexity of the models, which may be difficult to interpret based on regression coefficients alone, the results also are presented by simulating the expected value of the dependent variable or first differences (changes in the expected value of the dependent variable) based on the estimated coefficients (King, Tomz, and Wittenberg 2000).

For the victim-level analysis, the dependent variable is an indicator for whether a victim trended on Google or was protested. The initial models control for variables that account for whether victims are sympathetic and dangerous such as age in years as well as indicators for Black, Native American, Asian, Latino, and female. The models also include victim threat, which is an indicator for whether any coder characterized the victim threat level as 1 or 2, and other incident characteristics such as whether a death was recorded and occurred via gun or vehicle. Contextual variables account for organizational capacity and include place-level proportion Black, proportion Latino, social justice organizations per capita, and percent in poverty. Finally, the repressive political opportunity structure is measured by misconduct incidents per capita and an indicator for police departments under federal investigation. Twenty percent of the sample comes from cities with five or more victims; all models also control for fixed effects for these twenty-nine cities.[11] Two-thirds of the sample come from cities with only one or two officer-involved killings in 2016.

The regression results are presented in Table 2. The model in the first column presents the analysis of trending; the second column contains the results for protest. Because it is difficult to make sense of these coefficients in isolation, this section presents the expected probability that a victim trends on Google or gets protested conditional on certain characteristics of the incident, victim, and location. The expected probabilities are simulated based on the models in Table 2. At baseline, the indicators for recording, female, gunshot, and vehicle accident were set to zero. Contextual variables, such as the proportion Black, proportion Latino, percent in poverty, misconduct per capita, and social justice organizations per capita, are set at their mean values, while indicators for federal investigations and city fixed effects were set to zero.

3.2.3 Multivariate Analysis: Trending after an Officer-Involved Killing

Like the simple statistics presented earlier, multivariate analyses show that public attention to victims of officer-involved killings depend on victim race. Figure 3 presents the probability of trending on Google by race and threat level. Both the figure and the model in Table 2 show that Black victims are more likely to trend on Google than are White or Latino victims regardless of threat level.

[11] Los Angeles, Chicago, Houston, Phoenix, San Antonio, Albuquerque, Austin, Baltimore, Charlotte, St. Louis, Stockton, Atlanta, Bakersfield, Bronx, Denver, Indianapolis, Jackson, Norfolk, Oklahoma City, Orlando, Reno, San Bernardino, San Francisco, Dallas, Columbus, Philadelphia, Tucson, Tulsa, and Washington, DC.

Table 2 Results from logit regression. Robust standard errors below. White and male are excluded as the baseline categories. Models include fixed effects for the twenty-four cities with more than five victims.
Note: *p<0.1; **p<0.05; ***p<0.01

	Trended	*Protested*
Low-Threat	0.240*	1.532***
	0.137	0.272
Recording	0.436***	0.863***
	0.131	0.251
Age	–0.028***	–0.031***
	0.005	0.011
Black Victim	0.358**	2.198***
	0.181	0.346
Latino Victim	0.039	0.703
	0.204	0.46
Native American Victim	0.658	1.436**
	0.419	0.706
Asian Victim	0.850*	1.134
	0.454	0.834
Female Victim	0.599***	0.747
	0.231	0.507
Gunshot	1.277***	1.264**
	0.278	0.499
Auto Accident	0.334	–3.109**
	0.316	1.337
Federal Investigation	–1.020*	–0.164
	0.589	1.249
Percent in Poverty	–0.027***	0.005
	0.009	0.018

Table 2 (cont.)

	Trended	*Protested*
Proportion Black	0.29	–0.223
	0.461	0.778
Proportion Latino	0.076	–0.192
	0.395	0.761
Social Justice Orgs Per Capita	2,943.008**	4,693.193**
	1,160.96	2,072.51
Misconduct Incidents Per Capita	–9,909.477**	–7,328.77
	4,268.41	7,016.40
Constant	–0.256	–4.936***
	0.375	0.725
N	1271	1271

The simulations show that high-threat Black male victims are 4.9 and 5.6 percent more likely to trend than are high-threat Latino and White male victims, respectively. Similarly, low-threat Black male victims are about 5.6 and 6.4 percent more likely to trend on Google than are low-threat Latino and White male victims, respectively. The difference in trending between White and Latino victims is not statistically significant.

Other victim characteristics affect public attention as well. Gender has a large, statistically significant difference in the probability of trending across racial groups. For all groups, women killed in vehicle accidents are about 13 to 14 percent more likely to trend on Google than are men. Black women killed by gunshot are 13.5 percent more likely than Black men to trend on Google; the gaps are 14.5 and 14.4 percent for White victims and Latino victims, respectively. Age is statistically significant in the model as well: there is a statistically significant association between youth and trending on Google for victims of officer-involved killings. Deaths of young people are more likely to generate public attention.

Going back to Figure 3, victim threat level is not statistically significant at $p < .05$ in the models presented in Table 2; $p = .08$. Figure 3 suggests that across racial groups, high-threat victims are slightly less likely to trend on Google. The

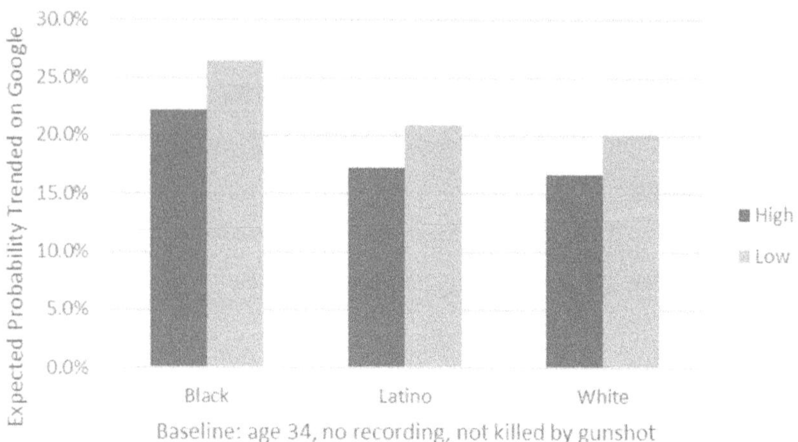

Figure 3 Probability of trending, by race and threat level. Expected probability of trending simulated based on estimates from the first model in Table 2.

likelihood that high-threat victims trend on Google is about 4 percent lower than that of low-threat victims. Interactions between Black and threat level and Black, threat level, and female are not statistically significant in additional models (not shown).

Incident characteristics such as manner of death and the existence of a recording also have large, statistically significant associations with receiving public attention, as Figure 4 shows. The intentional use of lethal force is important for traceability, and the probability that low-threat Black victims who are killed with a gun will trend on Google is 39.3 percent higher than that of Black victims who are killed by other means. A recording alone adds 9.1 percent to the probability that a low-threat Black victim will trend on Google. The changes in the probability that a victim trends on Google are of similar magnitude for White and Latino victims.

3.2.4 Multivariate Analysis of Protest after an Officer-Involved Killing

Multivariate analyses of the factors affecting protest also support the hypothesis: concerns about anti-Black discrimination make the race and threat level of victims important for understanding mobilization. Figure 5 shows the effect of victim threat on the likelihood that a victim's death is protested for Black, White, and Latino men, holding constant all other factors in the model. It is clear that, as expected, race and threat have a statistically significant association with

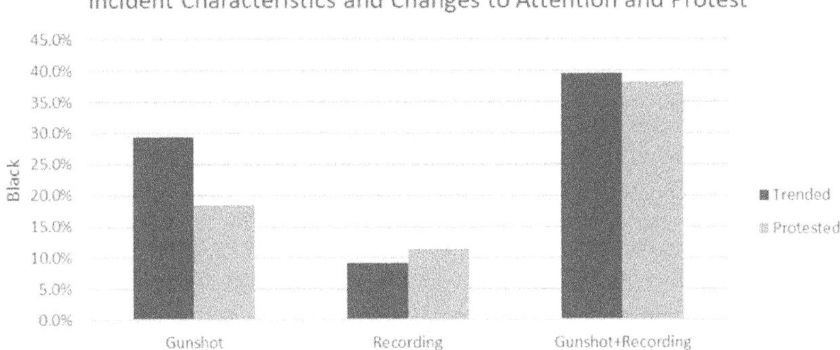

Figure 4 Probability that a victim is trending or protested, by incident characteristic. Expected probability of trending and protest simulated based on estimates from the models in Table 2.

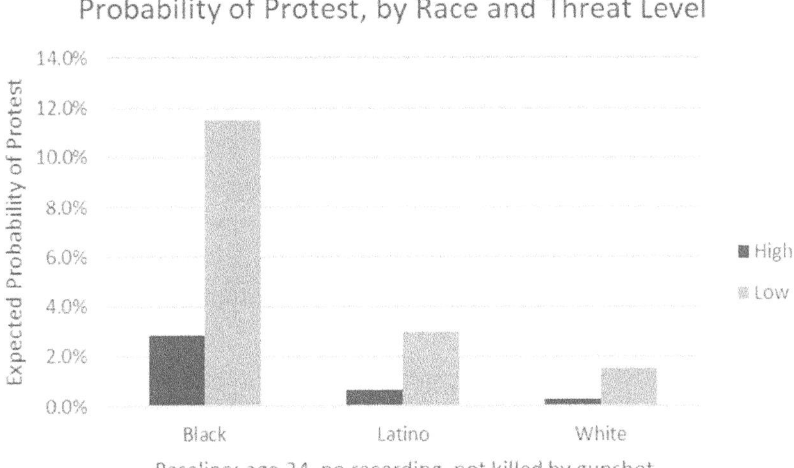

Figure 5 Expected probability of protest, by race and threat level. Expected probability of protest simulated based on estimates from the second model in Table 2.

the likelihood that a death is protested.[12] As shown in the figure, the probability of protest is highest for a death of a low-threat, Black male victim. Within each racial group, a high-threat victim is statistically significantly less likely to

[12] However, in additional models (not shown) the coefficient on the interaction between Black and low-threat is not statistically significant at traditional levels, nor are the interactions among Black, female, and low-threat.

generate protest than a low-threat victim. At each level of threat, Black victims are significantly more likely to have their deaths protested than Latino and White victims. The phenomenon noted previously in the bivariate data, that low-threat White male victims are less likely to generate protest than high-threat Black ones, remains statistically significant even in the multivariate analysis. The expected probability that deaths of low-threat Black male victims are protested is 10.0 percent higher than for White male victims and 8.5 percent higher than for Latino male victims. Deaths of low-threat Latino male victims are 1.5 percent more likely to be protested than deaths of similar White male victims. Similar relationships hold for high-threat victims, though the racial gaps are smaller: Black male, high-threat victims are 2.8 and 2.2 percent more likely to generate protest than their White and Latino counterparts, respectively. High-threat Latino and White men are nearly even; just 0.4 a percentage point separates the probability that their deaths are protested.

Delving further into the variables that strengthen traceability, it also is clear that deaths by gunshot and the availability of a recording are associated with a large, statistically significant increase in the probability that a victim's death is protested. Figure 4, which was introduced earlier, presents the change in the probability that a low-threat Black male generates protest when (a) they are killed by a gunshot, (b) there is a recording of the incident, or (c) both. Being killed by gunshot increases the probability that a low-threat Black male victim's death is protested by 18.4 percent with all other factors held constant. The presence of a recording adds 11.5 percent to the probability that a low-threat Black male victim's death is protested. The presence of a recording in combination with being killed by a gunshot adds 38.2 percent to the probability that a low-threat Black male victim's death is protested. Each of these changes is statistically significant.

Other victim characteristics also affect the likelihood that their death is protested. Gender is an interesting phenomenon and operates differently than with public attention. The coefficient on gender is not statistically significant in the model in Table 2. Looking first at the difference between low-threat male and female victims who were killed in car accidents, we see very little change in the probability of protest, regardless of racial group, because almost no one's death is protested in this group. Among Black victims, the difference in the probability of protest between men and women killed in car accidents was 1.1 percent; among Latino victims, 0.3 percent; among White victims, 0.1 percent. Alternatively, if we look at low-threat male to female gunshot victims, female victims are statistically significantly more likely to generate protest than male victims: the gap is 17.2 percent among Black victims, 5.1 percent among White victims, and 9.3 percent among Latino victims. Despite this pattern in the data, the interactions between female and vehicle and female and gun are not statistically significant.

To summarize, the analysis of victims of officer-involved killings suggests that concerns about anti-Black discrimination shape mobilization in the aftermath of incidents: Black victims killed after force was used without a legally relevant justification (such as when victims were not posing a threat to officers or bystanders) are the most likely to mobilize attention and protest. Although victim threat level was statistically significant for protest but not attention, race played an important role in determining both. Other factors associated with visibility, such as age and gender, or traceability, such as the manner and recording of deaths, mattered as well.

3.3 Observer-Level Analyses

Survey data provides additional evidence of the reactions of observers of officer-involved killings. The observer-level analyses join victim data from Fatal Encounters to the 2016 Collaborative Multi-racial Post-election Survey (CMPS). Questions for the CMPS were user-generated from a team of eighty-six social scientists, were fielded using an online platform, and were available in five languages. The total sample size was 10,145 and oversampled racial and ethnic minorities, with sample sizes of 3,003 Latino, 3,102 Black, 3,006 Asian, and 1,034 White. respondents The interviews were completed between December 3, 2016 and February 15, 2017.

Each analysis uses the timing of officer-involved killings relative to survey participation as a way of randomly assigning survey respondents to treatment and control conditions in order to make causal claims. For each analysis, the key causal variable is exposure to officer-involved deaths within one mile of the respondent's zip code. Respondents who have the value one on this treatment were exposed to officer-involved deaths before they took the survey, but not afterwards. Respondents who score zero on this treatment are in the control group: they were exposed to officer-involved deaths after they took the survey, but not before. The effects are analyzed for Black respondents under age forty, which is the median age of the Black sample in the CMPS, and for respondents of other races under age forty and older Black respondents. The effects of exposure are calculated for all victims, Black victims, trending or high-visibility victims, and low-threat victims.

Using the timing of the survey produced treatment and control groups that were balanced on dozens of covariates, including those related to individual demographic characteristics and community social and political context. No covariates were correlated with both the treatment assignment and any of the dependent variables.

Three dependent variables are considered in the following analysis. First, political interest is the "willingness to pay attention to politics possibly at the expense of other phenomena" (Lupia and Philpot 2005: 1122). It is measured by the CMPS question, "Some people are very interested in politics while other people can't stand politics. How about you? Are you . . . (1) Very interested in politics; (2) somewhat interested; (3) not that interested in politics; or (4) not at all interested in politics?" Second, voter turnout in the 2016 election is self-reported and measured using the question "Did you vote in the November 2016 election," but adds unregistered but eligible voters back into the "no" category for a total of 8,737 valid responses.[13] Finally, protest is an indicator for whether the respondent attended a protest in the last twelve months, where 1 = "Yes."

3.3.1 Officer-Involved Killings and Political Interest

The observer-level examination of political interest (discussed in greater detail in Burch 2022b) provides further evidence that concerns about anti-Black discrimination motivate the response to officer-involved killings.[14] The data fit the same pattern as that found by analyzing public attention to victims: Black victims are the most likely to generate interest among young Black CMPS respondents. As is the case with attention at the victim level, victim threat is not as important: as Figure 6 shows, exposure to all trending Black victims, regardless of threat level, significantly increases political interest. However, exposure to low-threat Black victims, regardless of whether they are trending, produces larger statistically significant effects on interest. In the "low-threat/high-visibility" condition, 53.3 percent of the control group is predicted to be "very" or "somewhat" interested in politics, compared with 69.5 percent of the treatment group. In the "all Black victims" condition, the gap between treatment and control is 7.1 percent but is not statistically significant. Only Black victims produce an effect: none of the conditions that test the effects of young Black respondents' exposure to victims of all races were statistically significant, regardless of victim threat level or visibility. Similarly, the effects on interest are isolated to observers who are disproportionately burdened or threatened by officer-involved killings: exposure to victims of officer-involved killings did not affect political interest among young observers in other racial groups or Black observers over age forty, regardless of the race, threat level, or visibility of the victim.

[13] It is worth noting that this analysis uses self-reported turnout, rather than validated turnout, which people may overreport (Silver, Anderson, and Abramson 1986). Also, using the November 2016 election as a reference may overestimate the turnout effect, as turnout effects may differ for midterm elections (Laniyonu 2019).

[14] More information can be found in the online appendix to this Element.

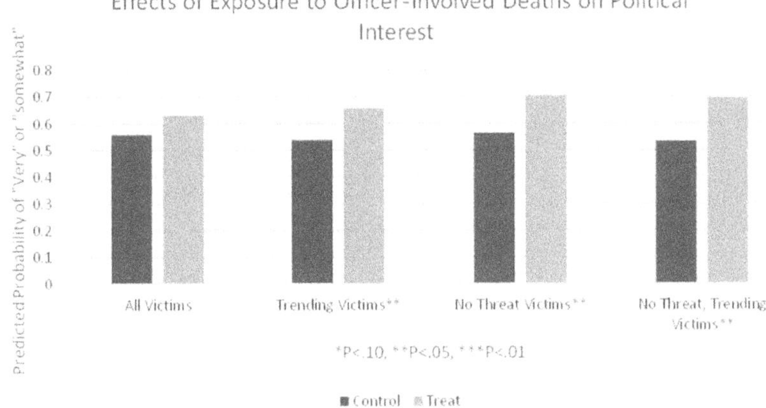

Figure 6 Estimated effect of officer-involved deaths on political interest, by victim threat and visibility. Predicted probabilities simulated based on estimates from the models in Appendix E (available online at www.cambridge.org/burch).

Source: Not All Black Lives Matter: Officer-Involved Deaths and the Role of Victim Characteristics in Shaping Political Interest and Voter Turnout" Perspectives on Politics Volume 20 Issue 4, pages 1174–1190.

3.3.2 Officer-Involved Killings and Voter Turnout

The pattern of results for self-reported voter turnout in the observer-level analysis (also discussed in greater detail in Burch 2022b) also supports the hypothesis: young Black respondents voted more when exposed to Black victims.[15] Threat and visibility again moderate this relationship, as expected. As Figure 7 shows, in the condition that considers exposure to all Black victims regardless of threat or visibility, the gap between the treatment and control groups is 8 percent and is not statistically significant. In the group exposed only to low-threat/high-visibility Black victims, the turnout gap is predicted to be 23 percent and is statistically significant at $p < .005$.

As is the case with the previous analyses, voter mobilization after an officer-involved killing is less likely to occur among non-Black observers and is less likely in response to non-Black victims. Among young Black CMPS respondents, the effects of exposure to victims of any race on self-reported voter turnout are still statistically significant, but with slightly smaller effect sizes. Exposure to victims of officer-involved deaths does seem to affect young people of other races politically, but in a direction that is opposite to that found among Black observers: exposure to all Black victims, trending Black victims, and low-threat Black victims (but *not* low-threat/high-visibility Black victims) produces statistically significant increases in turnout. Finally, exposure to victims of officer-involved deaths does not affect

[15] Please see the online appendix for more information.

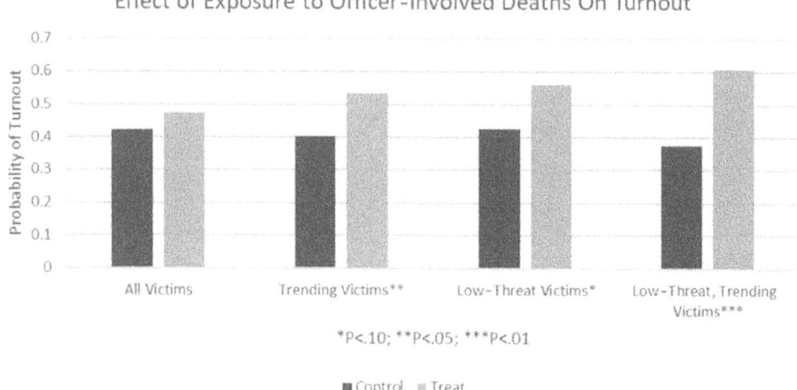

Figure 7 Estimated effect of officer-involved deaths on voter turnout, by victim threat and visibility. Predicted probabilities simulated based on estimates from the models in Appendix E (available online at www.cambridge.org/burch).

Source: Not All Black Lives Matter: Officer-Involved Deaths and the Role of Victim Characteristics in Shaping Political Interest and Voter Turnout" Perspectives on Politics Volume 20 Issue 4, pages 1174–1190.

self-reported voter turnout among Black respondents over age forty, perhaps because electoral participation in this group already is very high.

3.3.3 Officer-Involved Killings and Protest

The observer-level analyses of protest (appearing in Burch 2023) also confirm the victim-level analysis: protest of officer-involved killings is a rather limited phenomenon.[16] Most people are not mobilized to protest most victims of officer-involved killings, and in fact, for young Black observers, officer-involved killings appear to suppress protest in some cases.

The analysis of the effects of local exposure to officer-involved killings on respondents to the CMPS shows that most of the time, killings do not generate protest. There is no statistically significant effect of local exposure to officer-involved killings for most groups of respondents. This result is consistent with the theory: protest should happen only when people are mobilized in response to an identifiable grievance, and it is not clear that the public finds many officer-involved killings unjustified (this research design holds organizational context constant). For most groups, local exposure to an officer-involved killing still leads to null effects even when taking the race, visibility, and threat level of the victim into account: for White, Latino, and Asian respondents under age forty, and Black respondents over age forty, exposure to high-threat, low-visibility victims overall, and even Black victims in particular, does not affect the likelihood of attending a protest.

[16] Please see the online appendix for more information.

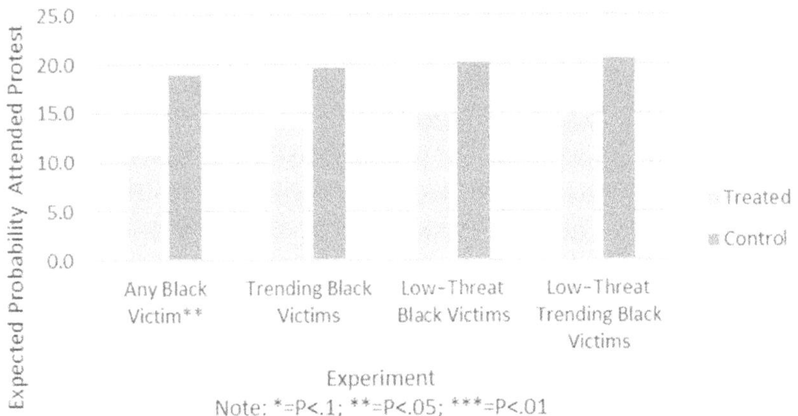

Figure 8 Expected protest attendance among Black respondents under age forty exposed to killings of Black victims within a mile of their zip code. Expected probability of attending protest simulated based on estimates from the models in Appendix E. (available online at www.cambridge.org/burch).

Source: Officer-Involved Killings and the Repression of Protest" Urban Affairs Review Volume 59 issue 2, pages 580–610. Year 2023

However, as shown in Figure 8, for Black respondents under age forty, exposure to a Black victim has a large, negative, and statistically significant effect on protest. The rate of attending a protest for young Black respondents who were exposed to an officer-involved killing of a Black person before taking the CMPS was 8.1 percent lower than that of young Black people who were exposed to officer-involved killings of Black people after the CMPS, a statistically significant difference. There are hints that grievances moderate the relationship between exposure and protest, at least among younger Black respondents. Taking victim threat level and visibility into account makes the repressive effect of officer-involved killings go away because the expected probability of protest in the treatment group increases in the conditions that take victim race, threat level, and visibility into account, while the expected probability of protest in the control groups remains relatively stable. This pattern is unique to young Black respondents exposed to Black victims, as the differences between the treatment and control groups are small for other groups exposed to Black victims regardless of whether victim characteristics are taken into account.

3.4 Summary and Discussion

As argued in Section 2, mobilization in response to officer-involved killings can be understood only in light of how a particular incident relates to the larger grievance against anti-Black discrimination. The data on mobilization, whether explored from the level of observers or victims, tell the same story: race of the victim and race of the observer are powerful predictors of public attention, protest, and voter turnout in response to an officer-involved killing. For all phenomena, victim threat, or the extent to which the killing is legally justified, moderates the mobilizing effects of race. Mobilization can occur after any officer-involved killing, particularly if victims are low-threat. However, mobilization is most likely to occur in circumstances when a killing can be attributed to anti-Black discrimination among people who are most threatened by or concerned by anti-Black racism.

The next section further explores the mediating effects of organizational infrastructure on mobilization. I argue that organizations are vital for understanding how grievances are constructed. They shape the visibility and perceptions of victims, as well as help individuals overcome the costs of organizing.

4 The Role of Organizations

Sections 2 and 3 discussed the importance of racial discrimination as a motivating grievance for mobilization against officer-involved killings. This conception of the grievance helps explain who will mobilize in response to officer-involved killings, and for whom they will act. However, political process models also discuss the importance of collective resources available for mobilization.

This section focuses on the importance of those collective resources for mobilizing in response to officer-involved killings. Traditionally, political scientists argue that organizations facilitate political involvement by reducing the costs or barriers of participating for their members, or by increasing motivation to participate (Klandermans and Oegema 1987; Skocpol and Fiorina 1999). I argue that organizations play a much larger role in mobilizing after an officer-involved killing, increasing participation not just for members, and not just by reducing costs. They do so in three ways: by increasing the visibility of victims, linking their deaths to racial discrimination, and overcoming barriers to collective action. Analyzing the data on officer-involved killings from 2016 supports this claim: public attention and protest are more likely when victims are killed in cities with a higher density of social justice organizations.

4.1 Changing the Calculus of Participation

Organizations have played an important role in mobilizing for victims of officer-involved killings. Black Lives Matter, which describes itself as a "a global organization in the US, UK, and Canada, whose mission is to eradicate White supremacy and build local power to intervene in violence inflicted on

Black communities by the state and vigilantes," is the most widely known of a set of organizations that routinely organize protests of victims of officer-involved killings (2021a). However, other groups such as the National Action Network have organized protests as well (McNamara 2020).[17]

McAdam argues that strong organizational networks are essential to sustained mobilization and the building of long-term social movements. Organizations are important because they provide "the associational network out of which a new movement emerges" (McAdam 1982:45). Social movements constitute a merger of established organizations and their members – mobilization involves recruiting blocs of people who are already organized rather than reaching out to isolated individuals (McAdam 1982:45). As Ransby writes, "Movement-building is forged in struggle, through people building relationships within organizations and collectives" (Ransby 2015). The lack of such relationships and infrastructure tends to produce "short term localized ephemeral outbursts and movements of protests such as riots" because organizing over the long term is so costly for individuals (McAdam 1982: 44).

Collective action requires resources to overcome costs, and "coordination and strategic effort is typically required in order to convert available pools of individually held resources into collective resources and to utilize those resources in collective action" (Edwards and McCarthy 2004: 116). For individuals, those costs may include the time needed to acquire information, register or vote, or attend a march (Verba, Schlozman, and Brady 1995). There also may be financial costs if a person has to take time off work to participate, or if they need to pay money to organize events (Verba, Schlozman, and Brady 1995). Participation also may be dangerous if activists are subjected to violence or surveillance (Earl 2011).

Organizations and other institutions can encourage activism primarily by rebalancing the calculus of individual civic participation in ways that make civic engagement and volunteering easier and more beneficial (Skocpol and Fiorina 1999). These groups can encourage participation by taking on the costs of fundraising, recruitment, and planning events, and can impart experience with past instances of collective action (Edwards and McCarthy 2004; Hansen 1985; Skocpol 1992). Organizations also may provide additional selective benefits to members such as t-shirts, lunches, discounts, or insurance in order to reward participation (Hansen 1985; Olson 1965). They may impose social pressure to participate or remind people of their duty to participate (Aldrich 1993). Organizations also can help with the formation of social identities, which

[17] But see also Taylor (2016).

are important for participating in social movements (Fisher, Dow, and Ray 2017; Klandermans and Oegema 1987).

Beyond the recruitment and mobilization of individuals, movements need leaders for thought leadership, such as agenda setting, expertise, and the prioritization of goals. Ransby argues:

> In order for activists to craft specific goals and demands wedded to a solid justice agenda built on the needs and aspirations of the most oppressed sectors of our communities, leadership, accountability, and organization are necessary ingredients (Ransby 2015).

More generally, organizations can provide moral resources such as "legitimacy, solidary support, sympathetic support, and celebrity" (Edwards and McCarthy 2004: 125). Organizations also are important sites for forging collective identities that help recruit and mobilize individuals (Polletta and Ho 2006; Taylor and Van Dyke 2004). Finally, established organizations and their networks facilitate the sharing of knowledge and resources across time and space (McAdam 1982: 46).

Some argue that the rise of the internet and social media have taken over some of the role that organizations traditionally played, particularly by reducing information and collective action costs. Bennett and Segerberg argue that these "digitally mediated collective action formations have frequently been larger; have scaled up more quickly; and have been flexible in tracking moving political targets and bridging different issues" (Bennett and Segerberg 2012). Activists also use social media during events to keep track of police and communicate with others (Cammaerts 2012).

Many local and national organizations undertake activities that reduce information and collective action costs in order to support mobilization against officer-involved killings. They do call for protests and other disruptive engagement, but typically when these groups call for action it is within the system (Tillery 2019). For instance, local organizations engage in mobilization campaigns focused on get-out-the-vote in support of police reform (Sago 2016; Woodly 2018). They may endorse or target political candidates, especially mayors and prosecutors, based on their dedication to punishing officers for killing citizens (Sago 2016; Woodly 2018). Several organizations, such as the Minnesota Freedom Fund, pay bail for people who are arrested for protesting police violence (Shaffer 2020).

There is evidence that the costs of mobilization matter for organizing against police violence. Nuamah finds that "mobilization fatigue" can be demobilizing to activists, even when they win (Nuamah 2021: 1125–1126). On the ground, some movement leaders note that some unjust killings may not get protested when a city "doesn't have 'rapid response' activists" to provide "the manpower to continually protest" (Ryan 2016). In addition to exhaustion, activists also face increased costs from repression. Researchers have shown that Black protesters specifically may face what Davenport refers to as "dissident-specific protest policing," which involves violence, arrest, or intimidation at protests (Davenport 2009; Davenport, Soule, and Armstrong 2011; Rafail, Soule, and McCarthy 2012). In 2020, protesters against police violence sometimes were met with officers in riot gear; beaten, gassed, and sprayed with chemical agents; and run down by police vehicles (ACLED 2020).

Thus, organizations play an important role in supporting the participation of activists as well as of ordinary citizens who want to mobilize against police violence. They reduce the costs of participating by disseminating information or paying bail. They also are the foundation for networks of activists who can share ideas and resources. Thus, organizations are important for strategic, long-term mobilization against officer-involved killings.

4.2 Increasing Victim Visibility

As discussed in Section 2, information about officer-involved killings is not readily available to the public. However, as Arnold notes, "Groups that suffer major costs under a particular governmental policy help to spread the word" (Arnold 1990: 49). Organizations do this important work of publicizing incidents and victims, increasing the level of public attention that victims receive. Their actions reduce the information costs associated with learning about officer-involved killings for activists as well as for the mass public.

Social movements and influencers can affect the level of attention received by victims of officer-involved killings (Hunt and Gruszczynski 2019). Activists associated with Black Lives Matter often serve this function, but other groups, including projects housed at the CATO Institute, the Washington Post, and FatalEncounters.org, also routinely collect and disseminate information about officer-involved killings. Black Lives Matter organizations, in particular, use social media to send thousands of tweets that express sadness and provide information about victims of officer-involved killings (Tillery 2019).

Women's deaths are less visible, especially those of Black women (Threadcraft 2017: 566). The #SayTheirNames campaign arose out of a concern that deaths of Black women at the hands of state and private actors are less visible than deaths of Black men and White women. Such invisibility is dangerous, they argue, because invisibility of victims implies that "certain deaths do not merit repercussions" (2021d).

Even solitary individuals can help increase visibility: the facts surrounding officer-involved deaths also may get out to the public through the actions of "networked microcelebrities," who are citizen-journalists using their social media presence for "reporting on the events, advocating for the cause, attempting to attract attention to the event and often also portraying a first-person, in-the-middle-of-it account of a highly charged, personally high-stakes situation" (Tufekci 2013). Bystander videos and accounts have played such a role in sparking attention to many deaths, including those of George Floyd and Philando Castile.

4.3 Tracing Killings to Racial Discrimination

As Woodly argues, social movement discourse rewrites "the common understandings present in the discursive field upon which political possibilities are considered" (Woodly 2015: 1). Organizations play an important and often overlooked role in facilitating mobilization: these groups do the discursive work of linking particular officer-involved killings to the larger movement against anti-Black discrimination. There are several kinds of organizations fighting against the police's use of excessive and lethal force in addition to the Movement for Black Lives, including left-wing and libertarian organizations such as the CATO Institute. However, many local Black activists are engaged in broader movements for economic and political liberation (Ransby 2018). For these activists, "protesting police is not the sole focus" of their work (Ryan 2016). Instead, they see themselves engaging in "a movement for Black liberation," which means "fighting to get more employment options, housing options, and food options in to Black neighborhoods" (Ryan 2016). Black Lives Matter describes itself as a "a global organization in the US, UK, and Canada, whose mission is to eradicate White supremacy and build local power to intervene in violence inflicted on Black communities by the state and vigilantes" (2021a). Black activists tie mobilization against police violence to a larger movement for Black liberation from White supremacy (Ransby 2018).

In this way, "cognitive liberation" (McAdam 1982) depends on the linkage of seemingly isolated incidents of officer-involved killings to a broader pattern of racial injustice. McAdam argues that this linkage is more likely to occur "under conditions of strong rather than weak social integration" (McAdam 1982: 50). Cognitive liberation is a collective process and is diffused through social networks, not developed independently by large numbers of individuals in isolation. Local and national organizations do this work of cognitive liberation intentionally, clearly linking officer-involved killings to racial oppression in their statements and literature. For example, Black Lives Matter explicitly links

Black deaths to racial oppression, writing that "Black Lives Matter is an ideological and political intervention in a world where Black lives are systematically and intentionally targeted for demise" (2021a).

In their statements and literature, organizations and activists also help make police actions traceable to racial discrimination. This work often involves producing counternarratives of victims and the events surrounding their killings to contradict those produced by public officials such as police or mayors. Social media is particularly important to the use of counternarratives as "discursive weapons" (Cammaerts 2012: 127). As the literature shows, perceptions of victim dangerousness play an important role in the construction of a particular killing as a grievance. Activists have engaged in a lively and contentious debate over the construction of victims as dangerous, altering "common sense understandings" of threat (Woodly 2015: 1). Threadcraft also writes:

> In the US context, it appears that the #BlackLivesMatter campaign has gained considerable ground in one aspect of a long-standing necropolitical struggle: it has gained ground not in stopping the production of dead bodies . . . but in the extremely important contest over the meaning of the bodies of the black dead . . . the #BlackLivesMatter campaign has been more successful in challenging the state's preferred meaning regarding the bodies of the dead. (Threadcraft 2017: 559)

For instance, in the cases of Botham Jean and Michael Brown, police departments tried to paint these victims of officer-involved killings as criminals, regardless of the relevance of their actions to their killings. Activists push back on attempts to frame victims of police violence as inherently dangerous, frequently questioning the role of race in framing perceptions of dangerousness. For instance, commentators have contrasted the routine arrests of several White mass murderers (such as Dylann Roof) with the immediate violence faced by Black people who were committing no crime at all (Pearl 2015). Pushing back on these characterizations of victims in this way could matter for whether people exposed to officer-involved killings attribute blame to the officer or to the victim, which should matter for protest.

The organizing framework of anti-Black discrimination is important to cognitive liberation for organizing against police violence involving Black victims. In contrast, there is no corresponding national movement of social justice activists and organizations routinely making these connections between police violence and systematic oppression for victims of other races killed by police. As a result, as the data from Section 3 show, protests and attention to victims of other races look like what McAdam characterized as "short term localized ephemeral outbursts" (McAdam 1982: 44). For instance, one unarmed White victim in the sample analyzed in Section 3 attracted a diverse group of organizers, including Black Lives Matter activists and groups carrying "White Lives Matter" signs and confederate flags to a protest, but did not produce a sustained movement (Esquivel 2016). Groups that might provide organizational support for victims of other races may not be capable of producing a sustained anti-violence movement: anti-fascist groups are loosely organized, and Occupy Wall Street describes itself as having been "crushed" by law enforcement and warns against copycat organizations on its website (2019a; Mogelson 2020).

4.4 Analysis of the Effects of Organizational Capacity

Given that organizations have consistently been observed doing the work of making killings visible, constructing their meaning, and organizing in response, we should expect to see effects of organizational presence on mobilization against police violence in the real world. However, previous research has found no support for the role of organizational capacity in explaining when protests of officer-involved killings occur (Streeter 2019; Williamson, Trump, and Einstein 2018). I think these null findings occurred because prior studies account for organizational capacity primarily by measuring the financial resources and size of minority groups in a city. Population size and density, race, poverty, income, and educational attainment have been included as measures of the resources available for mobilization (Streeter 2019; Williamson, Trump, and Einstein 2018). Williamson, Einstein, and Trump do include early NAACP mobilization as an indicator, but this variable captures organizational capacity from decades earlier (Williamson, Trump, and Einstein 2018). Neither study examines contemporary organizational capacity directly.

Instead, I measure organizational capacity directly using the place-level presence of social justice organizations per capita. These data on social justice organizations come from the 2016 IRS Master List of Exempt organizations. I incorporate this additional measure of organizational capacity into the analyses first presented in Section 3 in order to estimate the effects of local organizational capacity on the likelihood that a victim of an officer-involved killing will garner public attention or a protest. For consistency with past research, I also control for the place-level percent of residents in poverty and the proportion of residents who are Black or Latino in 2016 from the US Census Bureau.

The results of the multivariate regressions presented in Section 3 in Table 2 show that social justice organizations are important for victim visibility and mobilization in response to killings. The local density of social justice organizations has a positive, statistically significant effect on whether a victim trended on Google and on whether a victim was protested. I also find that the

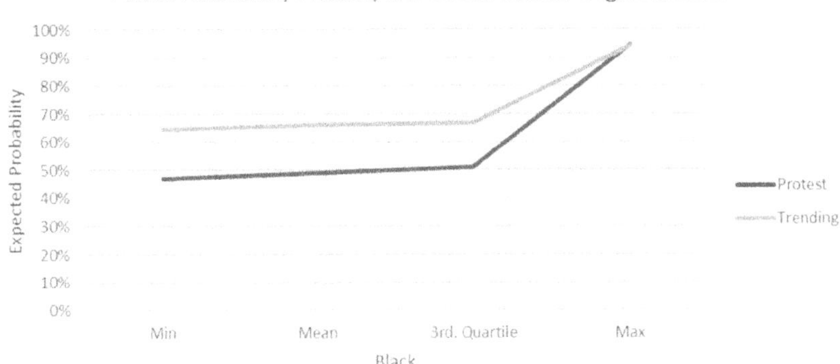

Figure 9 Probability of trending and protest, by the presence of social justice organizations. Expected probability of trending and protest simulated based on estimates from the models in Table 2.

resources available for mobilization matter for the likelihood that a victim will trend on Google even when measured by poverty rates: higher local poverty rates decrease the likelihood that a victim will trend on Google. Local poverty is not statistically significantly related to protest.

Figure 9 shows the association between the presence of social justice organizations in a city and the likelihood that a low-threat Black male victim generates public attention. As the data show, there is a modest, positive increase in the probability of trending on Google across most of the range of this variable. However, for cities with high levels of social justice organizations per capita at the upper end of the distribution, the expected probability of trending for a low-threat Black male victim is 94.2 percent. Local poverty also has a statistically significant relationship to trending on Google. Low-threat Black victims (with recording and killed by gunshot) have a higher probability of trending on Google in cities with low poverty than in cities with average poverty, a difference equal to 5.3 percent.

Figure 9 also shows the association between the presence of social justice organizations in a city and victim protest. As is the case with trending on Google, the presence of social justice organizations is associated with increases in the likelihood that a victim is protested. Again, across the majority of cities, the relationship between organizational capacity and protest is modest. However, in cities with high levels of social justice organizations, those organizations have a big effect on the likelihood that a victim is protested. Low-threat Black victims are almost certain to be protested when they are killed in cities with a high concentration of social justice organizations.

4.5 Discussion

The data show that social justice organizations are particularly important to the process of constructing and organizing the response to policing – McAdam's "cognitive liberation." By showing here that high concentrations of social justice organizations in a community increases both the likelihood of public attention and protest, this section provides evidence that the connection of police violence to a broader social movement matters for explaining the pattern of public reactions to victims of police violence. The data presented in this section support the claim that organizational capacity is important for producing the pattern of mobilization described in Section 3. The data presented in this section show that in most places when low-threat Black victims die in an officer-involved incident, especially when a gun is used, we should expect that about 70 percent will generate attention and about half will be protested. However, when dense networks of social justice organizations are present in a community, those same low-threat victims of officer-involved killings are almost certain to generate attention and protest.

The fact that organizations have such a big effect on mobilization demonstrates the importance of the Movement for Black Lives and the organizational capacity it generates. The activities of these groups may explain the sustained attention to Black victims of officer-involved killings relative to other groups. To Black activists, an officer-involved killing is not just about the specific incident, although, as the analysis in Section 3 shows, those factors do matter. Instead, it is the connection to a larger fight against racial discrimination that leads to mobilization. For Black victims, their connection to a larger movement for Black liberation can be driving increased attention and protest in ways that are not available to other groups whose victims are not connected to broader social movements against oppression. Streeter argues that the racial gap in protest can be attributed to racial differences in attitudes toward victims, finding that "Since White Americans are more likely to see the recipients of police violence as responsible for their own misfortune, they are more likely to believe that the officers 'did what they had to do'" (Streeter 2019: 76). However, this emphasis on individual attitudes neglects the importance of "cognitive liberation" and of social movements to shaping those attitudes.

5 Summary and Implications

Since the death of Michael Brown at the hands of Ferguson, Missouri police in 2014, mass mobilization after police kill citizens has been a prominent feature of American politics. However, the contours of that mobilization – who mobilizes, how they mobilize, and for whom they mobilize – has been less clear. This element engages these questions.

I argue that mobilization around officer-involved killings best can be understood as a function of concerns about anti-Black discrimination: people who are concerned about racism will respond to officer-involved killings that they attribute to racial discrimination. Concern about racism, I argue, is a function of threat, which is conditioned on Soss and Schram's definition of proximity as events felt "as a tangible presence affecting people's lives in immediate, concrete ways" (Soss and Schram 2007). Thus, young Black people are those most likely to mobilize after officer-involved killings, as they are the group most proximate to them (Edwards, Esposito, and Lee 2018). Killings attributable to anti-Black discrimination, I argue, are those killings of Black people by the use of force that are not attributable to any other legally relevant factor, such as victim dangerousness.

The analysis of data on individual victims and observers of officer-involved killings supports these claims, showing that mobilization after an officer-involved killing is most likely among young Black observers and in response to low-threat Black victims. Black victims of officer-involved killings were more likely to trend on Google and to get protested. Likewise, only exposure to deaths of Black victims consistently affected political interest, protest, and voter turnout among observers. And only young Black observers mobilized consistently after a killing in their communities.

Understanding the mobilization around officer-involved killings in this way has several implications for accountability, activism, and research. I discuss each below.

5.1 Implications for Accountability

As Aldon Morris argues, "A mobilized, protesting constituency is one that cannot be ignored and that in fact, becomes an important factor in the equation of power politics" (Morris 2017: 173). Young people are participating in politics in record numbers (Lopez 2022). Black youth electoral participation also has been increasing in recent elections (Rogowski and Cohen 2015). This research establishes that deaths of low-threat Black victims at the hands of police are important for increasing political participation and interest among young Black people. This increasing democratic participation in the pursuit of accountability is changing politics at the local, state, and national levels.

It is clear that the heightened attention to police violence is making a difference and has achieved some prominent victories. More progressive candidates are campaigning in local elections on platforms of police reform (Murray 2021). Protests of even a few exemplary victims have led to systemic changes across the country, such as bans on choke holds, that improve conditions more broadly. The election of progressive prosecutors to hold police departments accountable for uses of force in the wake of the deaths of Laquan MacDonald and other victims of officer-involved killings is another such change (Sklansky 2017; Smith et al. 2020). Other attempts at police reform have followed in the wake of the protests of George Floyd's death (Orenstein and Callaghan 2020). Such reforms may increase the likelihood that police departments and officers will be held accountable for officer-involved killings in the future.

However, while it is de rigueur to believe in the power of "The Resistance" to hold police departments and cities accountable, it is important to pay attention to the obstacles standing in the way of activists' ability to make a difference. This work highlights the limits of accountability through citizen mobilization, at least with respect to officer-involved killings. As this work has shown, most people who are killed in officer-involved incidents will not trigger public attention, protest, or other mobilization. Moreover, the pattern of protest and public attention uncovered in this analysis highlights a great inequality among victims. As the analysis shows, that inequality persists even after controlling for the victim's behavior. Mobilization is contingent on several other factors such as victim race, age, gender, manner of death, recording, and organizational context. Such inequality is concerning: deaths are less likely to get a public response if victims are asphyxiated rather than shot; if there are eyewitnesses rather than videos.

The inequity in who gets public attention and protest should matter if one thinks that attention and mobilization can lead to civil or criminal court resolutions or other forms of accountability in particular cases. If a just resolution depends on the kind of sustained advocacy work that has surrounded the Breonna Taylor case, for instance, then justice will not be done for many victims. The work of ensuring accountability in every case is a heavy burden to impose on activists, who "have jobs, families, and responsibilities keeping them from being able to organize a rally in response to every injustice they see" (Ryan 2016).

5.1.1 Official Narratives and Accountability

This Element argues that visibility matters for accountability. Cities and police departments also can make it more difficult for citizens and activists to hold them accountable for police violence by manipulating the visibility of officer-involved killings. Police departments and cities have a number of tools at their disposal to dampen public attention and political activity in response to officer-involved killings. Lack of transparency is one such avenue: as discussed earlier, police departments can fight the release of videos and coroners can attribute deaths not to restraints, TASERS, or police actions but to causes such as excited delirium (Harcourt 2015; O'Brien and Thom 2014; Truscott 2008). The data presented here show that these factors matter for public attention and mobilization.

As argued in Section 2, grievances are malleable. Public officials can and do produce narratives of officer-involved killings that attempt to minimize grievances by manipulating traceability. As Threadcraft writes, the state, in conjunction with the media, tries "to assure its citizens that it has produced the 'right kind' of dead" (Threadcraft 2017: 553):

> The state expends effort, uses its resources, to define how the subject lived and therefore what the subject was, thereby labeling a given subject as deserving of death, a subject whose proper embodiment is, in fact, a deceased body. (Threadcraft 2017: 558)

For instance, officials might issue statements that portray victims of police violence as dangerous, recasting incidents as legally justified even when the facts do not support that conclusion (Burch 2022a). For example, in its report on the Chicago Police Department, the Department of Justice highlights several instances of inaccurate descriptions of incidents by officers that were later undercut by video evidence. Here are two examples:

> In one incident captured on cell-phone video, an officer breaking up a party approached a man, grabbed him by the shirt, and hit him in the head with a baton. In his reports, the officer, using language very similar to that used in many other reports we reviewed, falsely claimed that the victim had tried to punch him. Before the video surfaced, the officer's supervisor had approved the use of force and the victim had pled guilty to resisting arrest. The officer has since been relieved of his police powers and is facing criminal charges for his conduct. In another video, a woman exited her car and placed her hands on her vehicle when officers threw her to the ground, hit her, and deployed a Taser against her. The video indicates that the officer's claim that she had refused to show her hands, thus justifying the force used, was false. Despite the existence of the video, IPRA deemed the force reasonable. (2017a: 39)

In these and other instances, the DOJ report describes a narrative structure that uses similar language across reports to say that the use of force was justified because suspects struggled with, hit or kicked officers, or refused officer commands, even when those claims were not true (2017a). Overall, my examination of initial statements by public officials that were issued in the aftermath of police killings of low-threat victims found that officials blamed victim behavior for the use of force in 80.3 percent of even these cases where such claims were not warranted (Burch 2022a).

5.1.2 Repression and Accountability

Accountability also is difficult because of the repression of activism and protest. Repression of activism in response to officer-involved killings is becoming increasingly common (Beydoun and Hansford 2017). Peaceful protesters of police violence have been threatened with violence and arrest at the highest levels of government (Rosenwald 2020). They have been met with officers in riot gear; beaten, gassed, and sprayed with chemical agents; and run down by police vehicles (ACLED 2020). Several people were killed at protests of police violence (Baker 2020). Dozens of people have been arrested at Black Lives Matter protests across the country, including eighty-four people protesting the death of Stefon Clark in Sacramento (2019b). Such arrests are costly (Earl 2005) and as plaintiffs allege in *The Dream Defenders et al. v. Desantis* (United States District Court, Northern District of Florida Case No.: 4:21cv191-MW/MAF), such state action may have a chilling effect on protest. The evidence suggests that in 2020, reports of violence at local protests increased staying-at-home behavior over and above concerns about the pandemic (Dave et al. 2020).

Protesters also may face violence and intimidation from nonstate actors (Tarrow 2011: 170). Armed counterprotesters have appeared at several protests (Okoren 2020; Shugerman and James 2021). Several protesters of police violence have been hurt or killed after they were run down by civilian vehicles (ACLED 2020). A new Florida law grants civil legal immunity to people who drive through protesters blocking a road, granting state cover to this form of violence from nonstate actors (Lemongello and Rohrer 2021).

Activists also face repression outside of protests. Federal, state, and local governments have routinely used surveillance and force to undermine social movements – COINTELPRO and its attempt to undermine civil rights activists is a prominent example of these operations (Davenport 2005; Earl 2011). Organizers of the Black Lives Matter movement, for instance, already have been labeled “Black identity extremists” and targeted by federal investigators (Beydoun and Hansford 2017). Some cities have targeted activists for greater surveillance as well (Gorner and Pratt 2019).

5.2 Implications for the Movement

The fact that mobilization against police violence is primarily focused on anti-Black discrimination means that deaths associated with injustice based on other characteristics, such as gender, class, or ethnicity, might fail to generate a political response. As was just discussed, the movement does not fight equally for all victims of officer-involved killings, even those who were not posing a threat. Partly, this is a matter of disproportionality: only Black victims are overrepresented among victims of officer-involved killings relative to their share in the population. However, the linking of deaths to a broader movement against anti-Black discrimination means that the movement against police violence has many of the same blind spots as earlier movements for Black equality, which often marginalized female, poor, and queer members of the community further (Cohen 2009). Threadcraft argues that it is not yet clear "how the movement can respond to existing hierarchies and prejudices in the wider black community" (Threadcraft 2017: 557).

For instance, violence against women may be less likely to generate a political response; Taylor notes the lack of public attention and mobilization in response to deaths of Black women at the hands of police in particular (Taylor 2016: 163). Threadcraft argues that this lack of attention and mobilization may stem from "the fact that the movement has relied on amplifying the spectacle of death in a context in which black women suffer from a severe spectacular violent death deficit" (Threadcraft 2017: 566). For instance, as I show in Section 3, officer-involved killings of women of all races look differently from those of men: most female victims are low-threat and tend to die in accidents. However, several have died as a result of intimate partners who were police officers, which even for Black women might not have been framed as racialized violence but rather as gendered violence (Richie 2012). Violence where women are bystanders in confrontations between police and male relatives or partners (such as Breonna Taylor's death, which occurred when police fired into her apartment after her boyfriend fired a warning shot during a no-knock raid) also may fail to generate a response because the women were not direct targets. However, the relatively few deaths where force was targeted against low-threat women were likely to generate a political response.

The focus on anti-Black discrimination as the motivating force might pose difficulties for building a broader, lasting cross-racial coalition against police violence. Taylor calls attention to backlash against the use of the hashtag #MuslimLives Matter in the wake of the deaths of Deah Barakat, Razan Abu-Salha, and Yusor Abu-Salha in Charlotte, North Carolina as an example of the forces limiting a broader coalition of oppressed people (Taylor 2016: 186–187). In Section 3, I describe several limitations on mobilization at the individual level. For instance, exposure to officer-involved killings did not consistently mobilize people of other races, even young people, regardless of the race or threat level of the victim. Likewise, exposure to deaths of people of different races seems to mobilize Black youth less than exposure to Black deaths.

Moreover, as Section 4 argues, the organizational infrastructure of communities is important to sustaining mobilization. As McAdam argues, movements stem from the merger of established organizations working toward a common goal. The lack of cross-racial mobilization at the observer level might reflect the lack of organizational resources on the ground. Cross-racial coalitions may exist only in communities where organizations representing different racial groups have a history of cooperating in the past. The prospects of a broader movement against police violence depend on changing these realities on the ground. George Floyd's disturbing death spurred a cross-racial mobilization that lasted several months, but that same outpouring of support has not been replicated at the same level for other victims.

5.3 Implications for Research

There are several implications of this work for future research on mobilization in response to officer-involved killings, and for social movements more broadly. The theory articulated in this Element relies heavily on the political opportunity structure tradition. However, unlike that tradition, which focuses more on the openness of the political system to explain movement activity, I argue for the centrality of grievances for explaining mobilization. Grievances are not just a necessary but static precursor to mobilization. Instead, I argue that grievances, and the salience of them, are malleable and subject to contestation in the political sphere. Paying attention to grievances, and their construction, and how they change over time, leads to an understanding of how particular incidents of police violence might precipitate political action. In this way, I link my work back to that of the Kerner Commission, which views acts of police violence as potential "precipitating events" in the longer fight for racial equality.

Viewing officer-involved killings in this way means that existing models of the effects of officer-involved killings on politics that do not account for incident characteristics, particularly the race, threat level, and visibility of victims, are underspecified or incomplete (see Cohen et al. 2019 as an example). Previous research that finds null effects of all officer-involved killings on politics should not be surprising; scholars should expect that only killings of certain victims, particularly low-threat and Black victims, should attract public attention and mobilization.

It also is important to pay attention to the role of organizational capacity and decisions in facilitating individual mobilization around officer-involved killings. Organizational infrastructure matters so much for the visibility and framing of incidents that it is important to consider it and explore it further in future research. In Section 4, organizational density makes such a difference to mobilization that it is essential for future research to take it into account. Specifically, it is important to study organizational decisions about which victims to support, which I do not examine here.

As a final note for future researchers, protest is not the only political response to officer-involved killings. In Section 3, exposure to officer-involved killings has much bigger effects on political interest and voter turnout than for protest. The Movement for Black Lives is most visibly associated with protest; however, many activists from the movement also are encouraging more institutionalized forms of political action such as voting (Lowery 2018; Tillery 2019; Woodly 2018). Rashida Tlaib and other progressives argue that outrage over the death of George Floyd increased Black voter turnout in the November 2020 general election. These findings lend credence to that claim and suggest that future research should look for evidence of electoral mobilization as well as protest.

References

1995. “Positional Asphyxia – Sudden Death,” edited by National Law Enforcement Technology Center. Department of Justice. Accessed June 27, 2023 at www.ojp.gov/library/publications/positional-asphyxia-sudden-death.

2017a. “Investigation of the Chicago Police Department.” United States Department of Justice, Civil Rights Division, and United States Attorney’s Office, Northern District of Illinois. Accessed June 27, 2023 at www.google .com/url?sa=t&rct=j&q=&esrc=s&source=web&cd=&ved=2ahUKEwiOleSbnLL_AhVFFFkFHSv9BtkQFnoECBwQAQ&url=https%3A%2F%2Fwww.justice.gov%2Fopa%2Ffile%2F925846%2Fdownload&usg=AOvVaw3VOSZzJUhO_vC8Yz7x0u_-.

2017b. “Sentencing Pushed Back for Meriden Teen Charged in Fatal August 2016 Crash.” August 10. Accessed June 27, 2023 at www.myrecordjournal.com/Archive/2017/08/MerSentenceDelayed-RJ-081017.

2019a. “Facts about Occupy Wall Street.” Accessed February 8, 2021 at http://occupywallst.org/.

2019b. “More Than 80 Arrested during Sacramento Police Shooting Protest.” *Al Jazeera*, March 5, 2019. Accessed February 18, 2021 at www.aljazeera .com/news/2019/3/5/more-than-80-arrested-during-sacramento-police-shooting-protest.

2020. The Dream Defenders et al. v. Desantis. United States District Court, Northern District of Florida.

2021a. “About Black Lives Matter.” Accessed February 8, 2021 at https://blacklivesmatter.com/about/.

2021b. “Charlamagne and Envy Debate over Lawfulness of Ma’Khia Bryant Shooting by Police.” Accessed June 27, 2023 at https://youtu.be/CXAsKxg8cO8.

2021c. “Fatal Force.” *The Washington Post*. Accessed February 8, 2021 at www .washingtonpost.com/graphics/investigations/police-shootings-database/.

2021d. “#SayHerName.” The African American Policy Forum. Accessed June 24, 2021 at www.aapf.org/sayhername.

ACLED. 2020. “Demonstrations & Political Violence in America: New Data for Summer 2020.” Accessed June 27, 2023 at https://acleddata.com/2020/09/03/demonstrations-political-violence-in-america-new-data-for-summer-2020/.

Aldrich, John H. 1993. "Rational Choice and Turnout." *American Journal of Political Science* 37 (1):246–278.

Appiah, Osei, Silvia Knobloch-Westerwick, and Scott Alter. 2013. "Ingroup Favoritism and Outgroup Derogation: Effects of News Valence, Character Race, and Recipient Race on Selective News Reading." *Journal of Communication* 63 (3):517–534.

Arnold, R Douglas. 1990. *The Logic of Congressional Action*. Yale University Press.

Aust, Charles F, and Dolf Zillmann. 1996. "Effects of Victim Exemplification in Television News on Viewer Perception of Social Issues." *Journalism & Mass Communication Quarterly* 73 (4):787–803.

Baker, Mike. 2020. "One Person Dead in Portland after Clashes between Trump Supporters and Protesters." *The New York Times*. Accessed December 13, 2021 at www.nytimes.com/2020/08/30/us/portland-trump-rally-shooting.html.

Barreto, Matt A, Sylvia Manzano, Ricardo Ramirez, and Kathy Rim. 2009. "Mobilization, Participation, and Solidaridad Latino Participation in the 2006 Immigration Protest Rallies." *Urban Affairs Review* 44 (5):736–764.

Bennett, W Lance, and Alexandra Segerberg. 2012. "The Logic of Connective Action: Digital Media and the Personalization of Contentious Politics." *Information, Communication & Society* 15 (5):739–768.

Bergesen, Albert. 1982. "Race Riots of 1967: An Analysis of Police Violence in Detroit and Newark." *Journal of Black Studies* 12 (3):261–274.

Beydoun, Khaled A, and Justin Hansford. 2017. "The F.B.I.'s Dangerous Crackdown on 'Black Identity Extremists'." *The New York Times*, November 15, 2017, Opinion. Accessed April 16, 2018 at www.nytimes.com/2017/11/15/opinion/black-identity-extremism-fbi-trump.html.

Birck, Morgan A. 2018. "Do You See What I See: Problems with Juror Bias in Viewing Body-Camera Video Evidence Note." *Michigan Journal of Race & Law* 24 (1):[i]–176.

Bobo, Lawrence D, and Devon Johnson. 2004. "A Taste for Punishment: Black and White Americans' Views on the Death Penalty and the War on Drugs." *Du Bois Review: Social Science Research on Race* 1 (01):151–180. doi: https://doi.org/10.1017/S1742058X04040081.

Boyle, Michael P, Mike Schmierbach, Cory L Armstrong, et al. 2004. "Information Seeking and Emotional Reactions to the September 11 Terrorist Attacks." *Journalism & Mass Communication Quarterly* 81 (1):155–167.

Braga, Anthony A, Christopher Winship, Tom R Tyler, Jeffrey Fagan, and Tracey L Meares. 2014. "The Salience of Social Contextual Factors in

Appraisals of Police Interactions with Citizens: a Randomized Factorial Experiment." *Journal of Quantitative Criminology* 30 (4):599–627.

Buchanan, Larry, Quoctrung Bui, and Jugal K Patel. 2020. "Black Lives Matter May Be the Largest Movement in U.S. History." *The New York Times*, July 3, 2020. www.nytimes.com/interactive/2020/07/03/us/george-floyd-protests-crowd-size.html.

Bunyasi, Tehama L, and Candis W Smith. 2019. "Do All Black Lives Matter Equally to Black People? Respectability Politics and the Limitations of Linked Fate." *Journal of Race, Ethnicity, and Politics* 4 (1):180–215.

Burch, Traci. 2022a. "Adding Insult to Injury: the Justification Frame in Official Narratives of Officer-Involved Killings." *Journal of Race, Ethnicity, and Politics* 7 (3):359–384.

Burch, Traci. 2022b. "Not All Black Lives Matter: Officer-Involved Deaths and the Role of Victim Characteristics in Shaping Political Interest and Voter Turnout." *Perspectives on Politics* 20 (4):1174–1190.

Burch, Traci. 2023. "Officer-Involved Killings and the Repression of Protest." *Urban Affairs Review* 59 (2):580–610.

Cammaerts, Bart. 2012. "Protest Logics and the Mediation Opportunity Structure." *European Journal of Communication* 27 (2):117–134. doi: https://doi.org/10.1177/0267323112441007.

Chong, Dennis, and James N Druckman. 2007. "Framing Theory." *Annual Review of Political Science* 10 (1):103–126. doi: https://doi.org/10.1146/annurev.polisci.10.072805.103054.

Cineas, Fabiola. 2021. "Why They're Not Saying Ma'Khia Bryant's Name." *Vox*, May 1, 2021. Accessed June 24, 2021 at www.vox.com/22406055/makhia-bryant-police-shooting-columbus-ohio.

Coan, Travis G, Jennifer L Merolla, Elizabeth J Zechmeister, and Daniel Zizumbo-Colunga. 2020. "Emotional Responses Shape the Substance of Information Seeking under Conditions of Threat." *Political Research Quarterly* 74 (4): 941–954. doi: https://doi.org/10.1177/1065912920949320.

Cobb, Jelani. 2016. The Matter of Black Lives. *The New Yorker*. March 6, 2016. available online: https://www.newyorker.com/magazine/2016/03/14/where-is-black-lives-matter-headed

Cohen, Cathy J. 2009. *The Boundaries of Blackness: AIDS and the Breakdown of Black Politics*. University of Chicago Press.

Cohen, Elisha, Anna Gunderson, Kaylyn Jackson, et al. 2019. "Do Officer-Involved Shootings Reduce Citizen Contact with Government?" *The Journal of Politics* 81 (3):1111–1123. doi: https://doi.org/10.1086/703539.

Conn, Jordan Ritter. 2020. "'She Loved Who She Was Becoming': Breonna Taylor and a Family's Fight for Justice." *The Ringer*, June 18, 2020. www.theringer.com/2020/6/18/21294510/breonna-taylor-louisville-police-black-lives-matter-protests.

Culhane, Scott E, John H Boman, and Kimberly Schweitzer. 2016. "Public Perceptions of the Justifiability of Police Shootings: the Role of Body Cameras in a Pre- and Post-Ferguson Experiment." *Police Quarterly* 19 (3):251–274. doi: https://doi.org/10.1177/1098611116651403.

Cullen, Francis T, Liqun Cao, James Frank, et al. 1996. ""Stop or I'll Shoot": Racial Differences in Support for Police Use of Deadly Force." *American Behavioral Scientist* 39 (4):449–460. doi: https://doi.org/10.1177/0002764296039004008.

Dave, Dhaval M, Andrew I Friedson, Kyutaro Matsuzawa, Joseph J Sabia, and Samuel Safford. 2020. *Black Lives Matter Protests and Risk Avoidance: the Case of Civil Unrest during a Pandemic*. National Bureau of Economic Research.

Davenport, Christian. 2005. "Understanding Covert Repressive Action: the Case of the US Government against the Republic of New Africa." *Journal of Conflict Resolution* 49 (1):120–140.

Davenport, Christian. 2009. "Regimes, Repertoires and State Repression." *Swiss Political Science Review* 15 (2):377–385.

Davenport, Christian, Sarah A Soule, and David A Armstrong. 2011. "Protesting While Black? The Differential Policing of American Activism, 1960 to 1990." *American Sociological Review* 76 (1):152–178.

Dawson, Michael C. 1995. *Behind the Mule: Race and Class in African-American Politics*. Princeton University Press.

Dukes, Kristin Nicole, and Sarah E Gaither. 2017. "Black Racial Stereotypes and Victim Blaming: Implications for Media Coverage and Criminal Proceedings in Cases of Police Violence against Racial and Ethnic Minorities." *Journal of Social Issues* 73 (4):789–807.

Earl, Jennifer. 2005. "'You Can Beat the Rap, But You Can't Beat the Ride': Bringing Arrests Back into Research on Repression." In *Research in Social Movements, Conflicts and Change (Research in Social Movements, Conflicts and Change, Vol. 26)*. Emerald Group Publishing Limited, Bingley, pp. 101–139. doi: https://doi.org/10.1016/S0163-786X(05)26004-4.

Earl, Jennifer. 2011. "Political Repression: Iron Fists, Velvet Gloves, and Diffuse Control." *Annual Review of Sociology* 37 (1):261–284. doi: https://doi.org/10.1146/annurev.soc.012809.102609.

Earl, Jennifer, Andrew Martin, John D. McCarthy, and Sarah A. Soule. 2004. "The Use of Newspaper Data in the Study of Collective Action." *Annual*

Review of Sociology 30 (1):65–80. doi: https://doi.org/10.1146/annurev.soc.30.012703.110603.

Edwards, Bob, and John D McCarthy. 2004. "Resources and Social Movement Mobilization." *The Blackwell Companion to Social Movements* 11:152–156.

Edwards, Frank, Michael H Esposito, and Hedwig Lee. 2018. "Risk of Police-Involved Death by Race/Ethnicity and Place, United States, 2012–2018." *American Journal of Public Health* 108 (9):1241–1248. doi: https://doi.org/10.2105/ajph.2018.304559.

Epp, Charles R, Steven Maynard-Moody, and Donald Haider-Markel. 2014. *Pulled Over: How Police Stops Define Race and Citizenship*. Chicago: University of Chicago Press.

Esquivel, Paloma. 2016. "Shooting of Unarmed White Teenager Has Racially Diverse Fresno Trying to Make Sense of Black Lives Matter." *Los Angeles Times*, July 21, 2016. Accessed February 8, 2021 at www.latimes.com/local/lanow/la-me-ln-fresno-shooting-20160721-snap-story.html.

Fatal Encounters. 2023. "Our Visualizations." Accessed March 13, 2023 at https://fatalencounters.org/our-visualizations/.

Felstiner, William L F, Richard L Abel, and Austin Sarat. 1980. "The Emergence and Transformation of Disputes: Naming, Blaming, Claiming." *Law and Society Review* 15 (3/4):631–654.

Fisher, Dana R, Dawn M Dow, and Rashawn Ray. 2017. "Intersectionality Takes It to the Streets: Mobilizing across Diverse Interests for the Women's March." *Science Advances* 3 (9):eaao1390.

Flanders, Chad, and Joseph Welling. 2015. "Police Use of Deadly Force: State Statutes 30 Years After Garner." *Saint Louis University Law Journal* 35:109.

Forliti, Amy. 2019. "Activists: Cop's Shooting of White Woman Treated Differently." Seattle Times, April 13, 2019. https://www.seattletimes.com/nation-world/nation/activists-cops-shooting-of-white-woman-treated-differently/.

Gelman, Andrew, Jeffrey Fagan, and Alex Kiss. 2007. "An Analysis of the New York City Police Department's 'Stop-and-Frisk' Policy in the Context of Claims of Racial Bias." *Journal of the American Statistical Association* 102 (479):813–823.

Glasford, Demis E. 2013. "Seeing Is Believing: Communication Modality, Anger, and Support for Action on Behalf of Out-Groups." *Journal of Applied Social Psychology* 43 (11):2223–2230.

Goldenberg, Jamie L, Tom Pyszczynski, Kern D. Johnson, Jeff Greenberg, and Sheldon Solomon. 1999. "The Appeal of Tragedy: a Terror Management

Perspective." *Media Psychology* 1 (4):313–329. doi: https://doi.org/10.1207/s1532785xmep0104_2.

Gorner, Jeremy, and Gregory Pratt. 2019. "Have You Spoken at a Chicago Police Board Meeting? The Police Know More about You Than You Realize." *Chicago Tribune*, July 24, 2019.

Greene, Kathryn, and Marina Krcmar. 2005. "Predicting Exposure to and Liking of Media Violence: a Uses and Gratifications Approach." *Communication Studies* 56 (1):71–93. doi: https://doi.org/10.1080/0008957042000332250.

Hacker, Jacob S, and Paul Pierson. 2005. "Abandoning the Middle: the Bush Tax Cuts and the Limits of Democratic Control." *Perspectives on Politics* 3 (1):33–53. doi: https://doi.org/10.1017/S1537592705050048.

Hansen, John Mark. 1985. "The Political Economy of Group Membership." *American Political Science Review* 79 (1):79–96.

Harcourt, Bernard E. 2015. "Cover-Up in Chicago." *The New York Times*, November 30, 2015, Opinion.

Heinecke, Jeannine. 2007. "'Knock, Knock.' 'Who's There?'" *Law Enforcement Technology* 34 (2):30–32.

Higginbotham, Evelyn Brooks. 1992. "African-American Women's History and the Metalanguage of Race." *Signs: Journal of Women in Culture and Society* 17 (2):251–274.

Hill, Evan, Ainara Tiefenthäler, Christiaan Triebert et al. 2020. "How George Floyd Was Killed in Police Custody." *The New York Times*, May 31, 2020. www.nytimes.com/2020/05/31/us/george-floyd-investigation.html.

Hoffner, Cynthia A., Yuki Fujioka, Jiali Ye, and Amal G. S. Ibrahim. 2009. "Why We Watch: Factors Affecting Exposure to Tragic Television News." *Mass Communication and Society* 12 (2):193–216. doi: https://doi.org/10.1080/15205430802095042.

Hollander, Jocelyn A. 2001. "Vulnerability and Dangerousness: the Construction of Gender through Conversation about Violence." *Gender & Society* 15 (1):83–109.

Huff, Jessica, Mauricio J Alvarez, and Monica K Miller. 2018. "Mock Juror Perceptions of Police Shootings: the Effects of Victim Race and Shooting Justifiability." *Applied Psychology in Criminal Justice* 14 (2):87–101.

Hunt, Kate, and Mike Gruszczynski. 2019. "The Influence of New and Traditional Media Coverage on Public Attention to Social Movements: the Case of the Dakota Access Pipeline Protests." *Information, Communication & Society* 24 (7):1024–1040. doi: https://doi.org/10.1080/1369118X.2019.1670228.

Hurwitz, Jon, and Mark Peffley. 2001. "Racial Polarization on Criminal Justice Issues: Sources and Political Consequences of Fairness Judgments." Annual Meeting of the American Political Science Association, San Francisco, CA.

Hurwitz, Jon, and Mark Peffley. 2005. "Explaining the Great Racial Divide: Perceptions of Fairness in the US Criminal Justice System." *The Journal of Politics* 67 (3):762–783.

Jefferis, Eric, Fredrick Butcher, and Dena Hanley. 2011. "Measuring Perceptions of Police Use of Force." *Police Practice and Research: an International Journal* 12 (1):81–96.

Johnson, Devon. 2008. "Racial Prejudice, Perceived Injustice, and the Black-White Gap in Punitive Attitudes." *Journal of Criminal Justice* 36:198–206.

Johnson, Devon, and Joseph B Kuhns. 2009. "Striking Out: Race and Support for Police Use of Force." *Justice Quarterly* 26 (3):592–623. doi: https://doi.org/10.1080/07418820802427825.

Jones, Jeffrey M. 2020. "Black, White Adults' Confidence Diverges Most on Police." Gallup. Accessed December 21, 2021 at https://news.gallup.com/poll/317114/black-white-adults-confidence-diverges-police.aspx.

Kahan, Dan M, David A Hoffman, and Donald Braman. 2009. "Whose Eyes Are You Going to Believe? *Scott* v. *Harris* and the Perils of Cognitive Illiberalism." *Harvard Law Review* 122 (3):837–906.

Kaye, Barbara K, and Thomas J Johnson. 2002. "Online and in the Know: Uses and Gratifications of the Web for Political Information." *Journal of Broadcasting & Electronic Media* 46 (1):54–71. doi: https://doi.org/10.1207/s15506878jobem4601_4.

Kerner, Otto, and John V Lindsay. 1968. Report of the National Advisory Commission on Civil Disorders. Washington, DC: National Advisory Commission on Civil Disorders, United States.

King, Gary, Michael Tomz, and Jason Wittenberg. 2000. "Making the Most of Statistical Analyses: Improving Interpretation and Presentation." *American Journal of Political Science* 44 (2):314–355.

Klandermans, Bert, and Dirk Oegema. 1987. "Potentials, Networks, Motivations, and Barriers: Steps towards Participation in Social Movements." *American Sociological Review* 52 (1987):519–531.

Knobloch-Westerwick, Silvia, Osei Appiah, and Scott Alter. 2008. "News Selection Patterns as a Function of Race: the Discerning Minority and the Indiscriminating Majority." *Media Psychology* 11 (3):400–417. doi: https://doi.org/10.1080/15213260802178542.

Knobloch-Westerwick, Silvia, and Matthias R Hastall. 2006. "Social Comparisons with News Personae: Selective Exposure to News Portrayals of Same-Sex and Same-Age Characters." *Communication Research* 33 (4):262–284.

Knobloch-Westerwick, Silvia, and Matthias R Hastall. 2010. "Please Your Self: Social Identity Effects on Selective Exposure to News about In- and Out-Groups." *Journal of Communication* 60 (3):515–535.

Kubey, Robert W, and Thea Peluso. 1990. "Emotional Response as a Cause of Interpersonal News Diffusion: the Case of the Space Shuttle Tragedy." *Journal of Broadcasting & Electronic Media* 34 (1990), 69–76.

Lalwani, Nikita, and Mitchell Johnston. 2020. "What Happens When a Police Officer Gets Fired? Very Often Another Police Agency Hires Them." *The Washington Post*, June 16, 2020. Accessed February 8, 2021 at www.washingtonpost.com/politics/2020/06/16/what-happens-when-police-officer-gets-fired-very-often-another-police-agency-hires-them/.

Laniyonu, Ayobami. 2019. "The Political Consequences of Policing: Evidence from New York City." *Political Behavior* 41 (2):527–558. doi: https://doi.org/10.1007/s11109-018-9461-9.

Lee, ByungGu, Jinha Kim, and Dietram A. Scheufele. 2016. "Agenda Setting in the Internet Age: the Reciprocity between Online Searches and Issue Salience." *International Journal of Public Opinion Research* 28 (3):440–455. doi: https://doi.org/10.1093/ijpor/edv026.

Legewie, Joscha, and Jeffrey Fagan. 2016. "Group Threat, Police Officer Diversity and the Deadly Use of Police Force." *Columbia Public Law Research Paper* (14-512). Accessed June 27, 2023 at https://scholarship.law.columbia.edu/cgi/viewcontent.cgi&article=2981&context=faculty_scholarship.

Lemongello, Steven, and Gray Rohrer. 2021. "DeSantis Signs 'Anti-Riot' Bill Into Law, Sparking Outcry from Democrats, Civil Rights Groups." *Orlando Sentinel*, April 19, 2021. Accessed December 9, 2021 at www.orlandosentinel.com/politics/os-ne-desantis-signs-anti-riot-bill-20210419-iltp27x5mzcbheeqvyhclhz2xq-story.html.

Lieberson, Stanley, and Arnold R. Silverman. 1965. "The Precipitants and Underlying Conditions of Race Riots." *American Sociological Review* 30 (6):887–898. doi: https://doi.org/10.2307/2090967.

Litman, Jordan. 2005. "Curiosity and the Pleasures of Learning: Wanting and Liking New Information." *Cognition and Emotion* 19 (6):793–814. doi: https://doi.org/10.1080/02699930541000101.

Lopez, Ashley. 2022. "Turnout among Young Voters Was the Second Highest for a Midterm in Past 30 Years." *NPR*, November 10, 2022. Accessed March 13, 2023 at www.npr.org/2022/11/10/1135810302/turnout-among-young-voters-was-the-second-highest-for-a-midterm-in-past-30-years.

Lowery, Wesley. 2018. "Police Are Still Killing Black People. Why Isn't It News Anymore?" *The Washington Post*, March 16, 2018. Accessed

April 17, 2018 at www.washingtonpost.com/outlook/police-are-still-killing-black-people-why-isnt-it-news-anymore/2018/03/12/df004124-22ef-11e8-badd-7c9f29a55815_story.html?utm_term=.611d836e6db2.

Lundman, Richard J, and Robert L Kaufman. 2003. "Driving While Black: Effects of Race, Ethnicity, and Gender on Citizen Self-Reports of Traffic Stops." *Criminology* 41 (1):195–220.

Lupia, Arthur, and Tasha S. Philpot. "Views from inside the net: How websites affect young adults' political interest." The Journal of Politics 67.4 (2005): 1122–1142.

Massie, Victoria M. 2016. "Native Americans Like Renee Davis Are Ignored When Police Brutality is Viewed as Black and White." Accessed February 5, 2020 at www.vox.com/identities/2016/10/25/13403290/renee-davis-police-violence-native-american.

Matthes, Jörg, and Christian Schemer. 2012. "Diachronic Framing Effects in Competitive Opinion Environments." *Political Communication* 29 (3):319–339.

McAdam, Doug. 1982. *Political Process and the Development of Black Insurgency 1930–1970*. Chicago: University of Chicago Press.

McIvor, David W. 2012. "Bringing Ourselves to Grief: Judith Butler and the Politics of Mourning." *Political Theory* 40 (4):409–436. doi:https://doi.org/10.1177/0090591712444841.

McNamara, Audrey. 2020. "Thousands Gather for 2020 March on Washington." *CBS News*, August 28, 2020. www.cbsnews.com/news/march-on-washington-dc-mlk-racial-equality-watch-live-stream-today-2020-08-28/.

Meares, Tracey L., Tom R. Tyler, and Jacob Gardener. 2015. "Lawful or Fair? How Cops and Laypeople Perceive Good Policing." *The Journal of Criminal Law and Criminology (1973–)* 105 (2):297–343.

Mettler, Suzanne, and Julianna Koch. 2012. "Who Says They Have Ever Used a Government Social Program? The Role of Policy Visibility." *The Journalist's Resource*. Accessed June 27, 2023 at www.google.com/url?sa=t&rct=j&q=&esrc=s&source=web&cd=&ved=2ahUKEwiujPG-5tr_AhXREGIAHak6B1UQFnoECAoQAQ&url=https%3A%2F%2Fjournalistsresource.org%2Fwp-content%252Fuploads%252F2012%252F09%252FPerceptionGovt-KochMettler-022812.pdf&usg=AOvVaw3im-Ck9GT8l6J5EjOVhreQ&opi=89978449.

Meyer, David S. 2004. "Protest and Political Opportunities." *Annual Review of Sociology* 30:125–145.

Michener, Jamila. 2019. "Policy Feedback in a Racialized Polity." *Policy Studies Journal* 47 (2):423–450.

Miller, Joanne M., and Jon A. Krosnick. "Threat as a motivator of political activism: A field experiment." Political Psychology 25.4 (2004): 507–523.

Mogelson, Luke. 2020. "In the Streets with Antifa." *The New Yorker*, October 25, 2020. www.newyorker.com/magazine/2020/11/02/trump-antifa-movement-portland.

Morris, Aldon. 2017. "The Future of Black Politics: Substance versus Process and Formality." In *Ethnic Politics and Civil Liberties*, 168–174. Routledge.

Mourtgos, Scott M, and Ian T Adams. 2020. "Assessing Public Perceptions of Police Use-of-Force: Legal Reasonableness and Community Standards." *Justice Quarterly* 37 (5):869–899.

Mullinix, Kevin J, Toby Bolsen, and Robert J Norris. 2020. "The Feedback Effects of Controversial Police Use of Force." *Political Behavior* 43 (2): 1–18.

Murray, Stephanie. 2021. "6 Cities Where Police Reform is Shaping the Race for Mayor." *Politico*, March 17, 2021.

Ng, Yu-Leung, and Xinshu Zhao. 2018. "The Human Alarm System for Sensational News, Online News Headlines, and Associated Generic Digital Footprints: a Uses and Gratifications Approach." *Communication Research* 47 (2):251–275. doi:https://doi.org/10.1177/0093650218793739.

Nuamah, Sally A. 2021. "The Cost of Participating While Poor and Black: toward a Theory of Collective Participatory Debt." *Perspectives on Politics* 19 (4):1115–1130. doi: https://doi.org/10.1017/S1537592720003576.

O'Brien, Anthony J., and Katey Thom. 2014. "Police Use of TASER Devices in Mental Health Emergencies: a Review." *International Journal of Law and Psychiatry* 37 (4):420–426. doi: https://doi.org/10.1016/j.ijlp.2014.02.014.

Okoren, Nicolle. 2020. "The Birth of a Militia: How an Armed Group Policies Black Lives Matter Protests." *The Guardian*. Accessed December 9, 2021 at www.theguardian.com/us-news/2020/jul/27/utah-militia-armed-group-police-black-lives-matter-protests.

Olson, Mancur. 1965. *The Logic of Collective Action*. Cambridge, MA: Harvard University Press.

Orenstein, Walker and Peter Callaghan. 2020. "The Legislature Just Passed a Police Reform Bill. What it Does – and Doesn't Do – To Reshape Law Enforcement in Minnesota." *MinnPost*, July 21, 2020. www.minnpost.com/state-government/2020/07/the-legislature-just-passed-a-police-reform-bill-what-it-does-and-doesnt-do-to-reshape-law-enforcement-in-minnesota/.

Owens, Michael Leo, and Hannah L. Walker. 2018. "The Civic Voluntarism of 'Custodial Citizens': Involuntary Criminal Justice Contact, Associational Live, and Political Participation." *Perspectives on Politics* 16 (4):990–1013.

Papacharissi, Zizi, and Alan M. Rubin. 2000. "Predictors of Internet Use." *Journal of Broadcasting & Electronic Media* 44 (2):175–196. doi:https://doi.org/10.1207/s15506878jobem4402_2.

Pasquier, Mathieu, Pierre-Nicolas Carron, Laurent Vallotton, and Bertrand Yersin. 2011. "Electronic Control Device Exposure: a Review of Morbidity and Mortality." *Annals of Emergency Medicine* 58 (2):178–188. doi: https://doi.org/10.1016/j.annemergmed.2011.01.023.

Patterson, Chase. 2014. "Don't Forget to Knock: Eliminating the Tension between Indiana's Self Defense Statute and No-Knock Warrants." *Indiana Law Review* 47 (2):621–643.

Pearl, Mike. 2015. "Why Are Some People Saying Dylann Roof Was Given Special Treatment When He Was Arrested?" *Vice*. www.vice.com/en_us/article/4wbnzd/why-are-some-people-saying-dylann-roof-was-given-special-treatment-when-he-was-arrested-623.

Peffley, Mark, and Jon Hurwitz. 2002. "The Racial Components of 'Race-Neutral' Crime Policy Attitudes." *Political Psychology* 23 (1):59–75.

Peffley, Mark, and Jon Hurwitz. 2010. *Justice in America: the Separate Realities of Blacks and Whites, Cambridge Studies in Public Opinion and Political Psychology*. Cambridge: Cambridge University Press.

Peffley, Mark, Jon Hurwitz, and Jeffery Mondak. 2017. "Racial Attributions in the Justice System and Support for Punitive Crime Policies." *American Politics Research* 45 (6):1032–1058.

Perkins, James E., and Martin J. Bourgeois. 2006. "Perceptions of Police Use of Deadly Force." *Journal of Applied Social Psychology* 36 (1):161–177. doi: https://doi.org/10.1111/j.0021-9029.2006.00056.x.

Pica, Emily, Chelsea L Sheahan, Joanna Pozzulo, and Craig Bennell. 2020. "Guns, Gloves, and Tasers: Perceptions of Police Officers and Their Use of Weapon as a Function of Race and Gender." *Journal of Police and Criminal Psychology* 35 (1):1–12.

Pierson, Emma, Camelia Simoiu, Jan Overgoor et al. 2020. "A Large-Scale Analysis of Racial Disparities in Police Stops across the United States." *Nature Human Behaviour* 4 (7):736–745.

Pierson, Paul. 1993. "When Effect Becomes Cause: Policy Feedback and Political Change." *World Politics* 45 (4):595–628.

Polletta, Francesca, and Mkai Ho. 2006. "Frames and Their Consequences." In Robert E. Goodin and Charles Tilly (eds.), *The Oxford Handbook of Contextual Political Analysis*, pp. 187–209. Oxford: Oxford University Press.

Rafail, Patrick, Sarah A Soule, and John D McCarthy. 2012. "Describing and Accounting for the Trends in US Protest Policing, 1960–1995." *Journal of Conflict Resolution* 56 (4):736–765.

Ransby, Barbara. 2015. "Ella Baker's Radical Democratic Vision." *Jacobin*, June 18, 2015. Accessed June 27, 2023 at https://jacobin.com/2015/06/black-lives-matter-police-brutality/.

Ransby, Barbara. 2018. *Making All Black Lives Matter: Reimagining Freedom in the Twenty-First Century*. University of California Press.

Ray, Rashawn. 2020. "Restructuring Civilian Payouts for Police Misconduct." *Sociological Forum* 35 (3): 806–812.

Richie, Beth E. 2012. *Arrested Justice*. New York University Press.

Rogowski, Jon C., and Cathy J. Cohen. 2015. Black Millennials in America. Online: Black Youth Project. Accessed June 27, 2023 at https://blackyouthproject.com/project/black-millennials-in-america-reports/.

Rosenthal, Aaron. 2020. "Submerged for Some? Government Visibility, Race, and American Political Trust." *Perspectives on Politics* 19(4), 1098–1114. doi:https://doi.org/10.1017/S1537592720002200.

Rosenwald, Michael S. 2020. "'When the Looting Starts, the Shooting Starts': Trump Quotes Miami Police Chief's Notorious 1967 Warning." *The Washington Post*, May 29, 2020. Accessed December 13, 2021 at www.washingtonpost.com/history/2020/05/29/when-the-looting-starts-the-shooting-starts-trump-walter-headley/.

Ryan, Jacob. 2016. "In the Weeks Following Darnell Wicker's Shooting, Few Public Protests." *89.3 WFPL*. wfpl.org/why-no-protests-in-days-following-darnell-wickers-death/.

Sago, Renata. 2016. "In the Black Lives Matter Era, an Effort to Elect More Diverse Prosecutors." *NPR*, November 5, 2016. Accessed November 25, 2020 at www.npr.org/2016/11/05/500714709/in-the-black-lives-matter-era-an-effort-to-elect-more-diverse-prosecutors.

Semenza, Daniel Charles, and John A Bernau. 2020. "Information-Seeking in the Wake of Tragedy: an Examination of Public Response to Mass Shootings Using Google Search Data." *Sociological Perspectives* 65 (1):07311214 20964785.

Shaffer, Claire. 2020. "Here's Where You Can Donate to Help Protests against Police Brutality." *Rolling Stone*. Accessed December 22, 2021 at www.rollingstone.com/culture/culture-news/george-floyd-protests-bail-funds-police-brutality-black-lives-matter-1008259/.

Shugerman, Emily, and Gerry Seavo James. 2021. "Three Injured as Rival Armed Militias Converge on Louisville." *The Daily Beast*. Accessed December 9, 2021 at www.thedailybeast.com/shots-fired-as-three-percenter-and-not-fucking-around-coalition-militias-face-off-in-louisville-kentucky.

Sigelman, Lee, Susan Welch, Timothy Bledsoe, and Michael Combs. 1997. "Police Brutality and Public Perceptions of Racial Discrimination: a Tale of Two Beatings." *Political Research Quarterly* 50 (4):777–791.

Silver, Brian D, Barbara A Anderson, and Paul R Abramson. 1986. "Who Overreports Voting?" *The American Political Science Review* 80(2): 613–624. doi:https://doi.org/10.2307/1958277.

Sklansky, David Alan. 2017. "The Changing Political Landscape for Elected Prosecutors." *Ohio State Journal of Criminal Law* 14:647–674.

Skocpol, Theda. 1992. *Protecting Mothers and Soldiers*. Cambridge, MA: Harvard University Press.

Skocpol, Theda, and Morris Fiorina. 1999. "Making Sense of the Civic Engagement Debate." In *Civic Engagement in American Democracy*, edited by Theda Skocpol and Morris Fiorina, 1–25. Washington, DC: Brookings Institute.

Skogan, Wesley G. 2006. *Police and Community in Chicago: a Tale of Three Cities*. New York: Oxford University Press.

Smith, Candace, Jake Lefferman, and Allie Yang. 2020. "Progressive Prosecutors Aim to Change the Criminal Justice System from the Inside." *ABC News*, October 1, 2020. Accessed June 27, 2023 at https://abcnews.go.com/US/progressive-prosecutors-aim-change-criminal-justice-system-inside/story?id=73371317.

Soss, Joe, and Sanford F Schram. 2007. "A Public Transformed? Welfare Reform as Policy Feedback." *American Political Science Review* 101 (1): 111–127. doi:https://doi.org/10.1017/S0003055407070049.

Stinson, Philip M, John Liederbach, and Steven L Brewer Jr. 2016. "Police Integrity Lost: a Study of Law Enforcement Officers Arrested." *Criminal Justice Faculty Publications* 63. Accessed June 27, 2023 at https://scholarworks.bgsu.edu/crim_just_pub/63.

Streeter, Shea. 2019. "The Racial Politics of Police Violence in the United States." Ph.D. thesis, Stanford University (28113079).

Stroud, Natalie Jomini. 2017. "Attention as a Valuable Resource." *Political Communication* 34 (3):479–489.

Tarrow, Sidney G. 2011. *Power in Movement: Social Movements and Contentious Politics*. New York: Cambridge University Press.

Taylor, Keeanga-Yamahtta. 2016. *From #BlackLivesMatter to Black Liberation*. Chicago: Haymarket Books.

Taylor, Verta, and Nella Van Dyke. 2004. "'Get Up, Stand Up': Tactical Repertoires of Social Movements." In *The Blackwell Companion to Social Movements*: 262–293. https://doi.org/10.1002/9780470999103.ch12.

Tennenbaum, Abraham N. 1994. "The Influence of the *Garner* Decision on Police Use of Deadly Force." *The Journal of Criminal Law and Criminology (1973–)* 85 (1):241–260.

Testa, Paul, and Bryce J Dietrich. 2017. "Seeing Is Believing: How Video Of Police Action Affects Criminal Justice Beliefs." Paper presented at the annual meeting of the American Political Science Association, San Francisco, CA. Accessed June 27, 2023 at https://convention2.allacademic.com/one/apsa/apsa17/index.php?program_focus=view_paper&selected_paper_id=1257179&cmd=online_program_direct_link&sub_action=online_program.

The Washington Post. 2023. "Fatal Force: 1093 People Have Been Shot and Killed by Police in the Past 12 Months." Accessed March 13, 2023 at www.washingtonpost.com/graphics/investigations/police-shootings-database/.

Threadcraft, Shatema. 2017. "North American Necropolitics and Gender: On# BlackLivesMatter and Black Femicide." *South Atlantic Quarterly* 116 (3): 553–579.

Tillery, Alvin B. 2019. "What Kind of Movement Is Black Lives Matter? The View from Twitter." *Journal of Race, Ethnicity and Politics* 4 (2):297–323.

Truscott, Amanda. 2008. "A Knee in the Neck of Excited Delirium." *Canadian Medical Association Journal* 178 (6):669–670. doi: https://doi.org/10.1503/cmaj.080210.

Tuch, Steven A., and Ronald Weitzer. 1997. "Trends: Racial Differences in Attitudes toward the Police." *The Public Opinion Quarterly* 61 (4):642–663.

Tucker, Michael Shawn. 2020. "When Law Enforcement Killed My Brother, There Was No Video." *The Washington Post*, June 15, 2020. www.washingtonpost.com/outlook/2020/06/15/matthew-tucker-riverside-county/.

Tufekci, Zeynep. 2013. "'Not This One' Social Movements, the Attention Economy, and Microcelebrity Networked Activism." *American Behavioral Scientist* 57 (7):848–870.

Verba, Sidney, Kay Lehman Schlozman, and Henry Brady. 1995. *Voice and Equality: Civic Voluntarism in American Politics*. Cambridge, MA: Harvard University Press.

Wade, Madison. 2021. "Minneapolis Police Press Release Tells Different Story of George Floyd Death." April 20, 2021. Accessed June 15, 2021 at www.abc10.com/article/news/local/george-floyd/video-chauvin-kneeling-george-floyd-reason-3-guilty-verdicts/103-7cf53df9-a725-413c-867b-04e41e114689.

Walker, Hannah L. 2014. "Extending the Effects of the Carceral State: Proximal Contact, Political Participation, and Race." *Political Research Quarterly* 67 (4):809–822. doi: https://doi.org/10.1177/1065912914542522.

Weaver, R Kent. 1986. "The Politics of Blame Avoidance." *Journal of Public Policy* 6 (4):371–398. doi: https://doi.org/10.1017/S0143814X00004219.

White, Ariel. 2016. "When Threat Mobilizes: Immigration Enforcement and Latino Voter Turnout." *Political Behavior* 38 (2):355–382. doi: https://doi.org/10.1007/s11109-015-9317-5.

White, Michael D, Justin Ready, Courtney Riggs et al. 2013. "An Incident-Level Profile of TASER Device Deployments in Arrest-Related Deaths." *Police Quarterly* 16 (1):85–112.

Williamson, Vanessa, Kris-Stella Trump, and Katherine Levine Einstein. 2018. "Black Lives Matter: Evidence That Police-Caused Deaths Predict Protest Activity." *Perspectives on Politics* 16 (2):400–415.

Woodly, Deva R. 2015. *The Politics of Common Sense: How Social Movements Use Public Discourse to Change Politics and Win Acceptance*. Oxford: Oxford University Press.

Woodly, Deva R. 2018. "An Electoral Vision for Black Lives." *Dissent* 65 (3):30–37.

Zhang, Yini, Dhavan Shah, Jordan Foley et al. 2019. "Whose Lives Matter? Mass Shootings and Social Media Discourses of Sympathy and Policy, 2012–2014." *Journal of Computer-Mediated Communication* 24 (4):182–202.

Zuckerman, Marvin, and Patrick Litle. 1986. "Personality and Curiosity about Morbid and Sexual Events." *Personality and Individual Differences* 7 (1):49–56. doi: https://doi.org/10.1016/0191-8869(86)90107-8.

Cambridge Elements

Race, Ethnicity, and Politics

Megan Ming Francis
University of Washington

Megan Ming Francis is the G. Alan and Barbara Delsman Associate Professor of Political Science at the University of Washington and a Fellow at the Ash Center for Democratic Governance and the Carr Center for Human Rights at the Harvard Kennedy School. Francis is the author of the award winning book, *Civil Rights and the Making of the Modern American State*. She is particularly interested in American political and constitutional development, social movements, the criminal punishment system, Black politics, philanthropy, and the post–Civil War South.

About the Series

Elements in Race, Ethnicity, and Politics is an innovative publishing initiative in the social sciences. The series publishes important original research that breaks new ground in the study of race, ethnicity, and politics. It welcomes research that speaks to the current political moment, research that provides new perspectives on established debates, and interdisciplinary research that sheds new light on previously understudied topics and groups.

Cambridge Elements ≡

Race, Ethnicity, and Politics

Elements in the Series

Walls, Cages, and Family Separation: Race and Immigration Policy in the Trump Era
Sophia Jordán Wallace, Chris Zepeda-Millán

(Mis)Informed: What Americans Know About Social Groups and Why it Matters for Politics
Marisa Abrajano, Nazita Lajevardi

Racial Order, Racialized Responses: Interminority Politics in a Diverse Nation
Efrén O. Pérez, E. Enya Kuo

Which Lives Matter?: Factors Shaping Public Attention to and Protest of Officer-Involved Killings
Traci Burch

A full series listing is available at www.cambridge.org/EREP

For EU product safety concerns, contact us at Calle de José Abascal, 56–1°, 28003 Madrid, Spain or eugpsr@cambridge.org.

www.ingramcontent.com/pod-product-compliance
Ingram Content Group UK Ltd.
Pitfield, Milton Keynes, MK11 3LW, UK
UKHW022145080726
473066UK00010B/765